STARK

KOMPAKT-WISSEN
ENGLISCH

Rainer Jacob

Wortschatz Oberstufe

STARK

ISBN 978-3-8490-1354-7

Inhalt

Fortsetzung siehe nächste Seite

Autor: Rainer Jacob

Vorwort

Liebe Schülerin, lieber Schüler,

Vokabeln sind das A und O einer Sprache. In allen Bereichen des Englischunterrichts – um Texte zu verstehen, Fragen zu beantworten, Kommentare und Meinungen differenziert auszudrücken, eine Sprachmittlung anzufertigen – sind gute Wortschatzkenntnisse unerlässlich.

Mit diesem Band aus der Reihe „Kompakt-Wissen“ können Sie Ihren aktiven und passiven Wortschatz erweitern und festigen. Die für Schularbeiten und die Matura wichtigen Vokabeln sind in übersichtlichen Wort- und Sachfeldern nach den **Themenbereichen** zusammengestellt. Außer der **deutschen Bedeutung** eines Wortes ist auch ein einprägsamer **Beispielsatz** angegeben, der die angemessene Verwendung in einem Kontext zeigt. Das erleichtert das Lernen und Behalten des Wortschatzes und macht feinere Bedeutungsunterschiede erkennbar, sodass die Vokabeln in entsprechenden Sprech- und Schreibsituationen selbstständig angewendet werden können. Angaben von **Synonymen und Antonymen** fördern zudem die Erweiterung des Wortschatzes.

Zum schnellen Nachschlagen und zur Orientierung steht ein umfangreicher Anhang zur Verfügung:

- ein Verzeichnis aller **Vokabeln des Grundwortschatzes** mit Übersetzung
- eine Zusammenstellung von Begriffen, für die im **britischen bzw. amerikanischen Englisch** unterschiedliche Wörter verwendet werden (z. B. „bill“ [BE] und „check“ [AE] für Rechnung)
- eine Liste der sogenannten **„falschen Freunde“**, die oft zu Fehlern verleiten („sensible“ heißt nicht „sensibel“).

Für die Erweiterung Ihres Wortschatzes und die Vorbereitung auf Schularbeiten wünsche ich Ihnen viel Erfolg.

Rainer Jacob

Vorwort

[illegible]

[illegible]

[illegible] Bedeutung eines Wortes [illegible] von Synonymen und Antonymen [illegible]

[illegible]

- [illegible]
- [illegible]
- [illegible]

[illegible]

[illegible]

Abkürzungsverzeichnis

AE	American English
BE	British English
e. g.	lat. exempli gratia = for example
esp.	especially
etw.	etwas
GB	Great Britain
i. e.	lat. id est = das heißt
jdm.	jemandem
jdn.	jemanden
Pl.	Plural
s.b.	somebody
Sg.	Singular
sl.	Slang
s.o.	someone
sth.	something
UK	United Kingdom, *hier:* Begriff ist nur in Großbritannien relevant
US	United States, *hier:* Begriff ist nur in den USA relevant
≠	Antonym
=	Synonym

Human relations

1 Partnership

vocabulary	dt. Bedeutung	English sentence	syn/opp
(to) become engaged	*sich verloben*	Mary has become engaged to John.	
cohabitation	*Zusammenleben ohne Trauschein*	Cohabitation has become more widespread.	
divorce	*Scheidung*	Britain has the highest divorce rate in the EU.	≠ marriage
domestic violence	*Gewalt in der Ehe, häusliche Gewalt*	Unfortunately, incidents of domestic violence are on the increase.	
engaged	*verlobt*	having agreed to marry s.b.	
engagement	*Verlobung*	an agreement to marry	
marriage	*Heirat, Ehe*	They can look back on 25 years of marriage.	≠ divorce
(to) marry	*heiraten*	She would only marry for love, not for money.	≠ to divorce
mixed marriage	*gemischte Ehe*	a marriage in which partners belong to different races	
same-sex marriage	*gleichgeschlechtliche Ehe*	Legislation to allow same-sex marriage in England was passed in 2013.	= gay marriage
(to) propose	*einen Heiratsantrag machen*	He was afraid that if he proposed she might refuse.	
single	*ledig*	Women remain single longer today.	≠ married
women's centre/shelter	*Frauenhaus*	a place for women who have become victims of domestic violence	

2 Family

vocabulary	dt. Bedeutung	English sentence	syn/opp
abortion	*Abtreibung*	A law was passed permitting abortion in the first 90 days of pregnancy.	≠ fertilisation
(to) adopt a child	*ein Kind adoptieren*	Couples who cannot have children of their own often wish to adopt a child.	
adoption	*Adoption*	The young mother gave up her baby daughter for adoption.	
(to) bear a child	*ein Kind gebären*	to give birth to a child	
birth-control	*Geburtenkontrolle, Verhütung*	Without proper birth-control there will be many more mouths to feed.	
(to) bring up children	*Kinder erziehen, aufziehen*	My grandmother brought up five children.	= to rear, to raise
(to) care for children	*Kinder betreuen*	Caring for children is a fulltime job.	
child abuse	*Kindesmisshandlung*	A recent TV documentary about child abuse made viewers aware of the problem.	= ill-treatment, mal-treatment, neglect
child care	*Kinderbetreuung*	Firms are improving child care facilities.	
child minder	*Tagesmutter*	Many working parents cannot afford a child minder.	= babysitter
child molestation	*Kindesmissbrauch*	An American superstar was accused of child molestation.	
childbirth	*Entbindung*	His wife died in childbirth.	

vocabulary	dt. Bedeutung	English sentence	syn/opp
children's/child's allowance	*Familienbeihilfe*	A legitimate or illegitimate child, stepchild or adopted child is entitled to children's allowance.	
(to) conceive (a child) conception	*(ein Kind) empfangen* *Empfängnis*	She conceived her first child at 17.	
contraception	*(Empfängnis-) Verhütung*	the practice and methods of preventing a woman from becoming pregnant	
delivery	*Entbindung*	an easy/difficult delivery	
delivery room/ ward	*Entbindungs-station*	She was taken to the delivery room straight away.	= maternity ward
expectant mother	*werdende Mutter*	a pregnant woman	
family allowance	*Kinder-/Familien-beihilfe*	amount of money that is given to a mother/father	
foster child	*Pflegekind*	a child who is taken care of by a couple who are not his/her legal parents	
(to) give birth to a child	*ein Kind gebären*	Sarah gave birth to her second child at 29.	= to bear a child
(to) have a baby	*ein Kind bekommen*	Women are deciding to have babies later in life.	
illegitimate (child)	*unehelich(es Kind)*	born to parents who are not married to each other	≠ legitimate
latchkey child	*Schlüsselkind*	a child of working parents who has to look after him-/herself until the parents come home from work	
maternity	*Mutterschaft*	The government has doubled the maternity grant.	= motherhood

vocabulary	dt. Bedeutung	English sentence	syn/opp
maternity leave	*Mutterschutz*	An expectant mother is entitled to take maternity leave before and after the birth of her child.	
only child	*Einzelkind*	Only children are often spoilt (*verzogen*).	
parental leave	*Kinderkarenz*	Simon took parental leave when his wife started to work again.	= family leave
patchwork family	*Familie, in der Kinder von verschiedenen Eltern aufwachsen*	The number of patchwork families is on the increase.	
pregnancy	*Schwangerschaft*	The increase in teenage pregnancies has alarmed sociologists and educators.	≠ miscarriage (*Fehlgeburt*)
pregnancy unplanned ~/ unwanted ~	*Schwangerschaft, ungewollte ~*	unplanned pregnancy/ unwanted pregnancy	
pregnancy test	*Schwangerschaftstest*	A pregnancy test can be carried out within a few days after conception.	
pregnant to be ~/ to get ~/ to become ~	*schwanger ~ sein, ~ werden*	Mrs Miller is pregnant with her fourth child.	
problem child	*Sorgenkind*	Doris Lessing's novel 'The Fifth Child' is about how a family copes with a problem child.	
single mother/ father, parent	*allein erziehende(r) Mutter/ Vater, Alleinerziehende(r)*	Tom is a single father of two and works full time.	

vocabulary	dt. Bedeutung	English sentence	syn/opp
skip-generation family	*Familie, in der die Kinder von den Großeltern erzogen werden*	a family in which children are raised by their grandparents	
(to) start a family	*eine Familie gründen*	Jennifer and Henry started a family when they were still teenagers.	
stepmother stepfather	*Stiefmutter Stiefvater*	Cinderella is mistreated by her stepmother and elder sisters.	
(to) support a family	*eine Familie ernähren*	Jeremy, who is 17 and still goes to school, doesn't earn any money and therefore cannot support a family.	= to sustain
surrogate mother/ motherhood	*Ersatzmutter/ Leihmutter Ersatzmutterschaft*	Couples who cannot have children seek the help of a surrogate mother to bear their child.	

3 Housekeeping

vocabulary	dt. Bedeutung	English sentence	syn/opp
breadwinner	*Brotverdiener*	Not every husband is prepared to give up his role as breadwinner.	= wage earner
chores	*(lästige) Hausarbeit*	to do the chores	= household tasks, jobs, responsibilities
(to) confine	*darauf beschränken*	Women in developing countries are confined to their traditional roles as wives, mothers, and homemakers.	= to restrict, to limit

vocabulary	dt. Bedeutung	English sentence	syn/opp
convenience food	*Fertiggericht*	Some young couples prefer to buy convenience food.	
domestic	*Haus-*	connected with the home or family	
domestic help	*Haushaltshilfe*	Many American families employ undocumented immigrants as domestic helps.	
domestic science	*Hauswirtschaftskunde*	Jamie O'Connor always earned top marks in Domestic Science.	
household appliances	*Haushaltsgeräte*	Household appliances have freed us from labour-intensive chores.	= household devices, gadgets
housekeeping (to) do housekeeping	*Haushaltsführung* *sich um den Haushalt kümmern*	taking care of a house, especially shopping and managing money	
housekeeping money	*Haushaltsgeld*	the money used to buy food, cleaning materials etc.	
housework (to) do housework	*Hausarbeit* *~ machen*	After returning from the office I have to do some housework.	
labour-intensive	*arbeitsintensiv*	Many labour-intensive chores have been associated with housework.	
monotonous	*eintönig*	never changing	≠ varied
repetitive	*sich ständig wiederholend*	Modern machines like dishwashers have freed us from repetitive jobs in the house.	= tedious, boring, dull

4 Women's lib

vocabulary	dt. Bedeutung	English sentence	syn/opp
equal opportunities	*Chancengleichheit*	Thanks to the feminist movement women are achieving equal opportunities.	
feminist movement	*Frauenrechtsbewegung*	The feminist movement which began in the sixties has profoundly changed women's lives.	
woman suffrage	*Wahlrecht für Frauen*	Woman suffrage was achieved in the first half of the 20th century.	
women's libber	*Frauenrechtlerin*	The Australian women's libber Germaine Greer published her controversial book 'The Female Eunuch' in 1970.	= feminist, women's liberationist, women's rightist
women's liberation movement/ women's lib	*Frauenrechtsbewegung*	The women's liberation movement seeks equal rights for women.	

Multi-cultural society

1 Immigration

vocabulary	dt. Bedeutung	English sentence	syn/opp
abode right of abode	*Aufenthalt* *Wohn-, Aufenthaltsrecht*	In 1971 Commonwealth citizens lost their right of abode in the UK.	
(to) accelerate	*beschleunigen*	The immigrants accelerated the economic growth of the country.	= to quicken, to speed, to facilitate
(to) advance	*voranbringen, fördern*	to bring or move forward, to raise to a higher rank	= to promote ≠ to hold back
advanced	*fortschrittlich*	A number of immigrants came from countries with advanced political and economic institutions.	= progressive
adverse	*widrig, feindlich, ungünstig, nachteilig*	The settlers had to cope with adverse weather conditions.	= hostile, unfavourable, bad; ≠ favourable
alien	*fremd, ausländisch; Ausländer*	a person of another race or nation or born in a foreign country	= foreign(er), strange(er)
(to) alienate	*entfremden*	to make s.o. feel isolated	
ancestor	*Vorfahr*	a person or a member of the family living in an earlier generation	= forebear ≠ descendant
ancestry	*Abstammung*	In the New World, a man's horizons would not be artificially limited by ancestry, class or religion.	
appalling	*erschreckend, entsetzlich*	The majority of American Indians live in appalling conditions.	= awful, dreadful, shocking

vocabulary	dt. Bedeutung	English sentence	syn/opp
approximately	*ungefähr*	Between 1815 and 1860 approximately five million people emigrated to America.	= about, roughly
(to) argue	*sich für etw. aussprechen*	The senator argued for a different immigration policy.	= to call for, to support
aspiration	*Bestrebung, Hoffnung, Ehrgeiz*	s.o.'s hope to achieve sth.	= ambition
(to) assimilate	*anpassen, eingliedern*	It is sometimes very hard for newcomers to assimilate into the new society.	
asylum	*Asyl*	the protection granted by a state, for example to a political refugee	
asylum seeker	*Asylsuchender*	s.o. looking for protection abroad	
(to) counsel	*beraten*	to give s.o. advice	= to advise
deportation	*Ausweisung*	The deportation of illegal immigrant has been made easier.	
descendant	*Nachfahre, Nachkomme*	a person or a family member living in a later generation	≠ ancestor
desperate	*verzweifelt*	being in a bad or frightening situation	
(to) detain	*festhalten, warten lassen*	The illegal immigrants were detained by the police for 24 hours.	
(to) diminish	*sich verringern, abnehmen*	The numbers of native Indians diminished rapidly as white settlement advanced.	= to decrease
disconcerting	*beunruhigend*	Many US citizens find the high number of immigrants to their country disconcerting.	

vocabulary	dt. Bedeutung	English sentence	syn/opp
distinct	*verschieden, deutlich*	New York City alone has more than 170 distinct ethnic communities.	= different,
diverse	*verschiedenartig, gemischt*	Intermarriage produced a population of diverse blood.	= mixed; promiscuous; varied
diversity	*Verschiedenheit*	The US is a multicultural society marked by unparalleled diversity.	= variety
Ellis Island	*Ellis Island*	From 1892 until 1943 Ellis Island served as the main entry point for immigrants by sea to the US.	
(to) emigrate	*auswandern*	to leave one's country	
entry procedure	*Einreise-, Aufnahmeverfahren*	Entry procedures at Ellis Island were frightening for many newcomers.	
(to) estimate	*abschätzen*	Experts estimate that the number of immigrants will increase even more.	
ferry boat	*Fährschiff, Fähre*	a (small) ship to transport people over a short distance	
filthy	*schmutzig*	extremely dirty	
flight (to) flee	*Flucht* *fliehen, flüchten*	fleeing or trying to escape	
founding fathers	*Gründerväter*	The founding fathers of the United States were the members of the American Constitutional Convention of 1787.	
freedom of worship	*Religionsfreiheit, freie Religionsausübung*	From the days of the Pilgrims men have come to America in search of freedom of worship.	

vocabulary	dt. Bedeutung	English sentence	syn/opp
frontier	*Grenze, Grenzgebiet*	the line or area separating two countries US: borderline between civilization and wilderness	= border
gateway	*Tor*	Ellis Island was the gateway to the US.	
green card	*Aufenthaltserlaubnis*	a permit allowing a foreign national to live and work permanently in the US	
homeland	*Heimatland*	Many Jamaicans left their homeland because they couldn't find any work.	
immigrant	*Einwanderer*	Numerous immigrants came to the USA in search of liberty.	
immigration act	*Einwanderungsgesetz*	An immigration act was passed to reduce the number of people who wanted to live and work in the UK.	= bill, law
immigration quota	*Einwanderungsquote*	From 1924 to 1968 immigration to the US was regulated according to an immigration quota system.	
indignation	*Entrüstung*	angry criticism, often expressed because of unfair treatment	
ineligible	*ungeeignet*	Political activists were declared ineligible for immigration.	= unsuitable, unfit
influx	*Zustrom*	Many British politicians tried to stop the influx of people from Commonwealth countries.	= inflow

vocabulary	dt. Bedeutung	English sentence	syn/opp
interpreter	*Dolmetscher*	Most immigrants needed the help of an interpreter to understand the questions of the immigration officers.	
(to) intimidate	*einschüchtern*	Sweatshop employers often intimidated their illegal workers.	= to scare, to frighten
(to) invigorate	*stärken*	The contributions of the immigrants invigorated the nation's life.	= to strengthen, to reinforce, to intensify
landmark	*Wahrzeichen*	The Statue of Liberty is one of New York's famous landmarks.	
(to) line up	*sich anstellen*	to stand and wait in a queue	
low-status job	*Arbeit mit geringem Ansehen, niedrige Arbeit*	When immigrants first arrived they often had to accept low-status jobs.	
(to) lure	*anlocken*	Adventurers were lured to the US because of the open unexplored wilderness of the country.	
melting pot	*Schmelztiegel*	Americans have always believed that their country was a melting pot of nations.	
migrant worker	*Wanderarbeiter, Gastarbeiter*	a worker who travels to wherever he can find work	
migration **(to) migrate**	*(Völker-)Wanderung* *(ab-, aus-) wandern*	Sociologists study migration to analyze the effects it has on the social structure.	
minority	*Minderheit*	the smaller part of a group	

vocabulary	dt. Bedeutung	English sentence	syn/opp
misfit	*Außenseiter*	a person who is different from the masses and does not fit into society	= outsider
multi-racial	*gemischtrassig*	The US is a multi-racial society.	
native	*einheimisch*	The American Indians are the native population of the US.	
native language	*Muttersprache*	Hispanic immigrants want to preserve their native language and speak only Spanish to their children.	= mother tongue
(to) naturalize naturalization	*einbürgern* *Einbürgerung*	to give a foreigner the citizenship of a country	
newcomer	*Neuankömmling*	a person who has recently arrived	
nightmare	*Alptraum*	an unpleasant and terrible dream	
ordeal	*schwere Prüfung, Qual, Tortur*	For many immigrants the examinations at Ellis Island were an ordeal.	
outlaw	*Geächteter, Bandit*	a person who has broken the law	
penniless	*mittellos, ohne Geld*	Illegal and undocumented immigrants from Mexico arrived in the States completely penniless.	
(to) persecute	*verfolgen*	Racists persecute a minority out of prejudice, hatred or envy.	
pledge	*Versprechen, Gelöbnis*	a formal promise	

vocabulary	dt. Bedeutung	English sentence	syn/opp
prejudiced	*voreingenommen*	Older immigrants were prejudiced against the newcomers from Eastern Europe.	
prospect	*Aussicht*	The immigrant had the prospect of earning a living for himself and his family.	= chance, expectation, hope
(to) provide	*zur Verfügung stellen*	East Asian migrants have their own businesses and provide employment.	= to give, to offer
quota	*Kontingent, Quote*	The 1924 Johnson Act established quotas for immigration based on the number of former nation-als of each country in the United States.	
refuge	*Zuflucht*	a safe place which protects from danger or trouble	= shelter
refugee	*Flüchtling*	a person who has had to leave his/her country or home, because of a war or for political or religious reasons	
relative	*Verwandter*	a member of one's family	
(to) relocate	*umsiedeln*	Young immigrant families were willing to pack their belongings and relocate to another part of the continent.	= move
resentment	*Abneigung, Groll, Missgunst*	Discrimination and resent-ment between ethnic groups are often still alive below the surface.	= ill-feeling, jealousy, grudge
reservation	*Vorbehalt*	East European immigrants were met with reservation.	

vocabulary	dt. Bedeutung	English sentence	syn/opp
restriction	*Ein-, Beschränkung*	Canada introduced severe restrictions on the number of immigrants.	
riches [Pl.]	*Reichtum, Reichtümer*	The search of riches and prosperity has brought millions to America.	= wealth
salad bowl	*Salatschüssel*	people of different races and cultural backgrounds living together in a nation	
(to) seek	*suchen*	Not all immigrants found what they sought.	
shelter	*Unterkunft*	a place giving protection from bad weather or danger	
(to) slow down	*verringern, verlangsamen*	The Immigration Bill of 1971 was passed to slow down the influx of people from Commonwealth nations.	
sweatshop	*Ausbeutungsbetrieb*	a small factory in which people worked in very bad conditions	
tide	*Flut, Zustrom*	In the 19th century a tide of immigration began bringing more than 40,000,000 persons into the country up to 1960.	= inflow, influx
undocumented	*ohne (Ausweis-) Papiere*	Employers in the sweatshops of the textile industry exploited many undocumented immigrants	= non-registered, illegal
xenophobia	*Ausländerfeindlichkeit*	Unfortunately, racism and xenophobia have always existed.	
yearning	*Sehnsucht*	a strong and urgent desire	

2 Multi-racial society

vocabulary	dt. Bedeutung	English sentence	syn/opp
(to) appal	*entsetzen, schockieren*	The brutality of the racial clashes has appalled the public.	= to shock
(to) assassinate	*ermorden*	M. L. King was assassinated in Memphis in 1968.	= to kill, to murder
(to be) barred (from)	*ausgeschlossen sein von*	Many blacks are still barred from equal opportunities at work.	= excluded from
citizen	*Staatsbürger*	In 1971 Commonwealth citizens lost their right of abode in the UK.	
citizenship	*Staatsbürgerschaft*	Immigrants can apply for citizenship after five years.	
civil right	*Bürgerrecht*	Blacks had been denied civil rights (for example the right to vote) for too long.	
civil rights movement	*Bürgerrechtsbewegung*	The Civil Rights Movement of the 1960s was led by Martin Luther King.	
clash	*Zusammenstoß*	Racial tension in Brixton ignited into violent clashes between blacks and the police.	
coloureds	*Farbige*	Coloureds make up 4.5 % of Britain's total population.	
conciliation	*Versöhnung, Besänftigung*	A conciliation committee was set up to settle disputes between black and white parents.	
delinquency	*Kriminalität*	criminal behaviour, usually of young people	

vocabulary	dt. Bedeutung	English sentence	syn/opp
(to) deny	*verweigern, leugnen*	Black children shouldn't be denied further (university) education.	
denial	*Ablehnung*		
discrimination	*unterschiedliche Behandlung, Benachteiligung*	Discrimination between men and women in employment is against the law.	
dispossessed	*Besitzlose, Enteignete*	people who don't own anything	
diversity	*Vielfalt*	Cultural diversity is one of the main characteristics of a multi-racial society.	= variety
enforcement	*Durchsetzung (eines Rechts oder Gesetzes)*	The Equal Opportunities Commission sees to the enforcement of the Equal Pay Act.	
equal opportunities	*Chancengleichheit*	Many blacks are still barred from equal opportunities at work.	
equal pay	*gleiche Bezahlung*	Women are entitled to equal pay with men when they are doing the same work.	
equality	*Gleichheit*	the same status for all members of a society	
ethnic	*Volks-*	There are many different ethnic groups in the USA.	
grudge	*Groll, Neid*	Black youths in the poorer area bear a grudge against rich whites.	= resentment
hate	*Hass*	The underprivileged masses in the black ghettos will develop deep feelings of hate towards white society.	= hatred
homeless	*Obdachlose*	people without a roof over their heads	

vocabulary	dt. Bedeutung	English sentence	syn/opp
(to) humiliate	*demütigen, erniedrigen*	make s.o. feel ashamed	
inferiority	*Minderwertigkeit*	the feeling of not being as good as others	
insoluble	*unlösbar*	sth. that cannot be solved or explained	
intervention **(to) intervene**	*Einmischung* *sich einmischen*	Critics of globalisation protest against the intervention of the industrialized states into the politics of developing countries.	
juvenile	*Jugend-*	juvenile delinquency	
liberation	*Befreiung*	Civil rights activists fight for the liberation of oppressed people everywhere.	= freeing
minority	*Minderheit*	The United Kingdom has a large Asian minority.	≠ majority
non-violent	*gewaltlos*	M. L. King adopted the means of non-violent protest from Mahatma Gandhi.	
(to) oppress **oppression**	*unterdrücken* *Unterdrückung*	All over the world racial minorities are oppressed.	= to suppress, to persecute
(to) populate	*bevölkern*	Brixton, a district in South London, is populated by black people, mostly from the West Indies.	
prejudice	*Vorurteil, Voreingenommenheit*	It is not only older people who have prejudices against foreigners.	

vocabulary	dt. Bedeutung	English sentence	syn/opp
(to be) prejudiced against	*Vorurteile haben gegenüber, voreingenommen sein gegen*	Too many people are still prejudiced against foreigners.	= biased
pursuit (to) pursue	*Streben, Verfolgung, Trachten* *verfolgen, streben*	Among the basic human rights are: life, liberty and the pursuit of happiness.	
race relations	*Rassenbeziehungen*	The problem of unemployment has made race relations worse in the past years.	
racial problem	*Rassenproblem*	There are serious racial problems between whites and blacks in big cities in Britain today.	
racial tension	*Rassenspannung*	Life in some districts of Los Angeles has become almost unbearable by crime and racial tension.	
resistance (to) resist	*Widerstand* *widerstehen, standhalten*	Resistance to teaching children in English and Spanish has increased in California.	= opposition
right to vote	*Stimmrecht*	Blacks were denied the right to vote for too long.	= suffrage, franchise
segregation racial ~	*Abtrennung, Absonderung, Rassentrennung*	In 1954, the Supreme Court decided that racial segregation in schools was against the constitution.	
Supreme Court [US]	*Oberster Gerichtshof (in den USA)*	the highest court of law	
(to) tackle	*fertig werden mit, anpacken (ein Problem)*	How will the mayor tackle the problem of the homeless and poor?	= to cope with, to manage

vocabulary	dt. Bedeutung	English sentence	syn/opp
tension	*Spannung*	Racial tension in Brixton ignited into violent clashes between blacks and whites.	
thug	*Schlägertyp, Rowdy*	a violent and often criminal person	
tolerance	*Duldung, Toleranz*	Tolerance is one of the most important values in society.	
troublemaker	*Unruhestifter*	a person who often causes difficulties or problems	
unalienable	*unveräußerlich*	The US Declaration of Independence guarantees the people's unalienable rights.	
unconstitutional	*verfassungswidrig*	The US Supreme Court ruled that racial segregation at schools was unconstitutional.	
underprivileged	*schlechter gestellt, unterprivilegiert*	The underprivileged masses provide a potential for conflict and riots.	
uninhabitable	*unbewohnbar*	impossible to live in	
violation	*Verletzung (eines Rechts)*	breaking a law, an agreement or a promise	

3 Civil rights

vocabulary	dt. Bedeutung	English sentence	syn/opp
(to) abuse	*missbrauchen; beschimpfen*	The managing director abused his position and authority.	= to exploit
(to) adhere	*festhalten an, befolgen*	Employers should adhere to civil rights laws.	

vocabulary	dt. Bedeutung	English sentence	syn/opp
adherence	*(An-)Haften, Festhalten*		
(to) affect	*sich auswirken*	to produce an effect on s.o. or sth.	
(to) affirm	*versichern, bekräftigen*	to state as a fact	
affirmative action	*Förderungsmaßnahme zugunsten von Minderheiten*	employing a black woman, a Muslim or a handicapped person before an equally qualified white person	
allegation	*Behauptung, Beschuldigung*	saying that s.o. has done sth. illegal or wrong	
(to) allege	*beschuldigen*		
(to) amend	*ändern, ergänzen*	The Voting Rights Act of 1965 was last amended in 1992.	
(to) appeal	*Berufung einlegen (vor Gericht)*	turning to a higher court to review the decision of a lower court	
arbitrary	*willkürlich*	A democratic country needs a judiciary which is independent of the arbitrary power of a president or prime minister.	≠ lawful, rightful, legitimate
(to) assign	*an-, zuweisen*	A special task force was assigned to investigate criminal offences.	
(to) assist	*helfen, unterstützen*	The department assists in the elimination of discrimination.	= to help, to support
assistance	*Unterstützung*		
attempt	*Versuch*	The new legislation is an attempt to bring about social justice.	

vocabulary	dt. Bedeutung	English sentence	syn/opp
basis	*Grundlage*	It is illegal to discriminate on the basis of race, sex or religion.	
clause	*Klausel, Bestimmung*	The equal protection clause of the 14th Amendment (1868) provides that "all persons born or naturalized in the United States … are citizens of the United States."	
complaint	*Beschwerde, Klage*	a statement that a product or a situation is unsatisfactory or unacceptable	
(to) conduct	*durchführen*	to conduct an experiment, a study, a survey	
(to) consult	*um Rat fragen; sich beraten*	to ask s.o. for his advice The members of the Amnesty groups consult each other on new projects.	
conviction (to) convince	*Überzeugung* *überzeugen*	Analysts expressed their conviction that immigrants contribute to the productivity of a country.	
conviction (to) convict	*Verurteilung* *überführen, verurteilen*	Anyone found guilty of a crime has the right of appeal against conviction.	
creed	*Überzeugung, Weltanschauung*	We believe in equal rights for all citizens regardless of race, colour, creed or politics.	= belief
damages	*Schadensersatz*	The pharmaceutical firm had to pay $ 5 million in monetary damages.	
(to) defend	*verteidigen*	A newly elected US president swears to defend the Constitution of the United States.	

vocabulary	dt. Bedeutung	English sentence	syn/opp
degradation	*Erniedrigung*	In the court case the two women complained about the degradation of sexual harassment (*Belästigung*).	
(to) deprive **deprivation**	*jdm. etw. nehmen* *Entbehrung*	Blacks were deprived of their civil rights for a long time.	≠ to grant
despair	*Verzweiflung*	Martin Luther King was never in despair about the just cause of his fight.	
disability	*Behinderung*	The new law improved the situation of some 43 million Americans who have one or more physical or mental disabilities.	
(to) discharge	*entlassen*	to tell s.o. that he can no longer work at his post/in his job	= to dismiss, to fire ≠ to hire, to contract
discrimination	*nachteilige Behandlung*	unfair treatment	
disparity	*Ungleichheit*	a great difference	≠ sameness, likeness, parity
(to) endure	*ertragen*	to bear an unpleasant situation	= to suffer, to tolerate
(to) enforce	*durchsetzen*	to put sth. into effect or operation	= to effect, to implement
enslavement	*Versklavung*	to make s.o. a slave	
(to) expand	*erweitern, ausdehnen*	In 1992 the Court expanded the powers of the states to regulate abortion.	
(to) file (a lawsuit)	*eine Klage einreichen*	Martin Luther King and his supporters filed a lawsuit against the city council of Montgomery.	

vocabulary	dt. Bedeutung	English sentence	syn/opp
(to) forbid	*verbieten*	to refuse to allow sth.	= to prohibit, to ban ≠ to permit, to allow
gender	*Geschlecht*	In 1928, Britain introduced the general right of voting; it ended all discrimination according to one's gender or social rank.	sex: refers to biological differences between men and women; gender: refers to cultural or social ones
guidance	*Beratung*	giving s.o. advice or information on how to solve a problem	
handicap	*Behinderung*	Discrimination on the basis of race, sex, handicap and national origin is illegal.	= disability
(to) harass **harassment**	*belästigen* *Belästigung*	The management issued a warning to male employees harassing women at work.	
incidence	*Auftreten, Vorkommen*	A rising incidence of sexual harassment was noted in the firm.	= occurrence
incident	*Zwischenfall, Ereignis*	"There has never been any incident of sexual harassment in our company", the manager said.	= case, event
(to) infringe	*verletzen, gegen etw. verstoßen*	Will the Net increase individual freedom – or infringe on privacy (*Privatsphäre*)?	
intervention **(to) intervene**	*Eingreifen* *einschreiten, intervenieren*	The president affirmed the right of the US to military intervention.	
(to) investigate	*untersuchen*	to examine carefully and thoroughly (*gründlich*)	

vocabulary	dt. Bedeutung	English sentence	syn/opp
lawsuit	*Klage*	a case before a court	
(to) monitor	*beobachten, kontrollieren*	CCTV cameras were installed to monitor public places.	
prejudice	*Vorurteil*	an unfair judgment of a person or a group of people, often caused by a lack of information	
prosecution	*strafrechtliche Verfolgung*	Crime prevention is better than crime prosecution.	
(to) prosecute	*belangen, anklagen*		
(to) read s.o. his/her rights	*jdn. über seine Rechte belehren*	The police must always read s.o. his/her rights before questioning.	
(to) register	*in das Wählerverzeichnis eintragen*	to enrol s.o. as a voter	
(to) require	*von jdm. etw. verlangen, jdm. etw. vorschreiben*	In all Montgomery buses, black passengers were required to sit at the back.	
requirement	*Bedingung, Voraussetzung*		
retaliation	*Vergeltung(smaßnahme)*	Martin Luther King rejected all acts of revenge and retaliation.	
(to) retaliate	*sich rächen*		
statute	*Gesetz, Statut*	a written law which was passed by parliament	= law
unlawful	*rechtswidrig*	against the law	
violation	*Verletzung*	Cloning of humans is regarded as a violation of human rights.	= an offence against
(to) violate	*verletzen*		
void	*nichtig*	The Supreme Court declares acts of Congress which violate the country's basic law as null and void.	= invalid

Crime

1 Crimes and offences

vocabulary	dt. Bedeutung	English sentence	syn/opp
abuse (to) abuse	*Missbrauch* *missbrauchen*	wrong or bad treatment	= mistreat-ment
armed robbery	*bewaffneter Raub*	using weapons to commit a robbery	
arson	*Brandstiftung*	the deliberate criminal act of setting fire to a building	
(to) beat up	*verprügeln*	Supporters of the visiting football team were beaten up by hooligans.	
(to) betray	*verraten*	Jesus was betrayed by Judas.	
bloodshed	*Blutvergießen*	The crusades caused massive bloodshed.	
bribery	*Bestechung*	corruption: accepting money in return for a favour	
burglary	*Einbruch, Einbruchdiebstahl*	entering a building illegally and stealing things from it	
CCTV (closed circuit television)	*Videoüberwachung*	a system of cameras used in many public places/ buildings to protect them from crime	
(to) cheat	*betrügen*	to act in a dishonest or unfair way in order to get an advantage for yourself	= to deceive, to trick, to swindle
child abuse	*Kindesmissbrauch*	Child abuse is a most disgusting crime.	

vocabulary	dt. Bedeutung	English sentence	syn/opp
(to) combat	*bekämpfen*	Severe sentences are expected to help combat crime.	= to fight, to battle, to struggle with
(to) condemn	*verdammen, verurteilen*	to express very strong disapproval	
(to) confiscate	*beschlagnahmen*	In the 1950s Salinger's novel *The Catcher in the Rye* was confiscated in many schools.	
conspiracy	*Verschwörung*	a secret plan to overthrow the government for example	= plot
convict (to) convict	*Verurteilter, Sträfling* *überführen, verurteilen*	Towards the end of the 18th century convicts were shipped to Australia as a punishment.	= criminal, offender, prisoner
conviction (to) convince	*Überzeugung; Verurteilung* *überzeugen*	a strong opinion or firm belief	≠ doubt
counsel for the defence	*Verteidiger*	lawyer who represents the defendant in a court case	
court	*Gerichtshof*	a place where trials or other law cases are held; a law court	
courtroom	*Gerichtssaal*	a room in which the sittings of the court are held	
credibility	*Glaubwürdigkeit*	He has lied so often before, his credibility is damaged.	= reliability, integrity
crime rate	*Kriminalitätsrate*	number of unlawful acts within a certain period of time	
crime-ridden	*von Verbrechen heimgesucht*	Black youngsters grow up in run-down and crime-ridden areas of big cities.	

vocabulary	dt. Bedeutung	English sentence	syn/opp
cross-examination	*Kreuzverhör (eines Zeugen)*	Under cross-examination the defendant admitted the crime.	
(to) cure	*heilen*	Drugs can kill as well as cure.	
curiosity	*Neugier*	the strong desire to know or be informed about sth.	≠ disinterest, indifference
custody	*Gewahrsam, Haft*	The suspect will remain in custody until his trial.	= care, supervision
cyberbullying	*Internetschikane, Cybermobbing*	Cyberbullying has become a widespread problem.	= cyberabuse
cybercrime	*Internetkriminalität*	Cybercrime is increasing.	= computer crime
cyberstalking	*über das Internet belästigen, nachstellen*	The officers who investigate cases of cyberstalking made several arrests.	
death penalty	*Todesstrafe*	The film *Dead man walking* is a protest against the death penalty.	= capital punishment
defence	*Verteidiger, Verteidigung*	a lawyer acting for an accused person	
delinquency	*Kriminalität*	bad or criminal behaviour	
(to) deny	*leugnen*	A big increase in drug-related crimes cannot be denied.	≠ to admit
	verweigern	African-American slaves were denied an education.	≠ to permit, to grant
deviance	*Abweichung*	strange and morally unacceptable behaviour	
(to) exact	*(dringend) fordern, eintreiben*	to demand (sometimes using force or threats)	
exposed	*ausgesetzt*	Children are exposed to hundreds of TV commercials every day.	

vocabulary	dt. Bedeutung	English sentence	syn/opp
(to) fiddle [sl.]	*manipulieren, betrügen*	The accountant fiddled the books of the company.	= to cheat, to con, to swindle
(to) forge forgery	*fälschen* *Fälschung*	to make a copy of sth. in order to deceive people	= to falsify, to counterfeit
fraud	*Betrug*	The journalist revealed numerous cases of fraud and corruption.	= deceit
identity theft	*(Online/Internet-) Identitätsdiebstahl*	Users of social networking sites have to take precautions against identity theft.	
intervention (to) intervene	*Eingreifen* *eingreifen, einschreiten*	The Republican president Ronald Reagan reduced government intervention in the private sector.	
investigation	*(offizielle, polizeiliche) Untersuchung*	An official investigation of the incident has been ordered by the prime minister.	= enquiry
juvenile delinquency	*Jugendkriminalität*	crime committed by young people	= youth delinquency
lawbreaker	*Gesetzesbrecher*	a person who does not obey the law	= criminal
moderate	*maßvoll, gemäßigt*	Martin Luther King's moderate views were not shared by all black leaders.	= reasonable ≠ extreme
(to) mug	*auf der Straße überfallen und berauben*	to rob s.o. (esp. with violence) in a public place	= to hold up, to rob, to ambush
murder	*Mord*	The defendant was convicted of murder in three cases.	= homicide, manslaughter
murderer	*Mörder*	Jack the Ripper is the most mysterious murderer in British criminal history.	= killer

vocabulary	dt. Bedeutung	English sentence	syn/opp
offender	*Übeltäter*	a person who breaks the law	= lawbreaker, delinquent
phishing	*ein Passwort erschleichen*	Criminals sent out faked emails phishing for people's username, pass-word etc.	
pickpocket	*Taschendieb*	person who steals from the pockets of others	
precaution	*Vorsicht(-smaß-nahme)*	sth. done in advance to avoid problems	
racketeer	*Gauner, Gangster*	a person who makes money through dishonest or illegal activities	
riot	*Krawall*	Race riots broke out in Los Angeles.	= disturbance, unrest
(to) rob	*be-, ausrauben*	The young criminal robbed the rich lady of her expensive jewellery.	
robber	*Räuber*	Kids used to play "cops and robbers".	
severe	*schwer wiegend, hart*	Will more severe sen-tences reduce the crime rate?	= strict, rigorous ≠ lenient, mild
shoplifting	*Ladendiebstahl*	to steal sth. from a shop while pretending to be a customer	
(to) stalk s.o.	*sich anschleichen, jmd. nachstellen*	to follow or approach (a celebrity, an enemy, an animal) without being seen	
(to) threaten threat	*(be-)drohen* *Bedrohung*	The gang threatened to beat him up if he didn't hand over his wallet.	
treason	*Hochverrat*	Mary, Queen of Scots, was executed for treason.	

vocabulary	dt. Bedeutung	English sentence	syn/opp
truancy (to) play truant	*Schulschwänzen* *(Schule) schwänzen*	staying away from school without good reasons	= to skip school
victim	*Opfer*	The Court ruled that he was the victim of discrimination.	
white-collar crime	*Wirtschaftsverbrechen*	stealing from a company or fiddling the books	

2 Drugs

vocabulary	dt. Bedeutung	English sentence	syn/opp
addict	*Süchtiger*	Drug addicts steal and rob to finance their drugs.	
addiction	*Sucht*	Drug addiction has increased in our affluent society.	
cocaine	*Kokain*	a powerful drug made from the coca plant	
dependence	*Abhängigkeit*	a steady need	= addiction, craving
designer drug	*synthetische Droge, Modedroge*	At parties designer drugs like 'ecstasy' or 'crystal meth' were passed round.	
distribution	*Vertrieb*	supplying or giving out things to people	= supply, delivery
dose	*Menge, Dosis*	an amount of a medicine to be taken at one time	
drug abuse	*Drogenmissbrauch*	Drug abuse among young people is on the rise.	
drug pusher	*Drogenhändler*	s.o. who sells drugs	= drug dealer
drug trafficking	*Drogenhandel*	dealing with drugs	

vocabulary	dt. Bedeutung	English sentence	syn/opp
drug-related	*mit Drogen in Zusammenhang stehend*	Theft and robbery are often drug-related crimes.	
(to) eradicate **eradication**	*ausrotten* *Ausrottung*	to get rid of sth. completely	= to eliminate, to wipe out
habit	*Gewohnheit*	Smoking is a filthy habit.	
harmful	*schädlich*	causing damage	= damaging, risky, unsafe
heroin	*Heroin*	a powerful drug made from poppies/opium	
(to) induce	*dazu bewegen*	Advertisements and commercials induce young people to spend their money.	= to tempt
intoxicating	*berauschend*	making you feel drunk	= stimulating
lethal	*tödlich*	The young man died after a lethal injection.	= deadly, fatal, mortal
narcotics	*Rauschgift*	Heroin and cocaine are narcotics.	
narcotics agent	*Rauschgift-fahnder*	Narcotics agents received special training to stop new ways of smuggling drugs into the country.	
overdose	*Überdosis*	too much of a drug taken at one time	
(to) peddle (drugs)	*mit Drogen handeln*	He was jailed for peddling cocaine on the streets.	
(to) sniff	*schnüffeln*	Kids of ten or even younger have begun sniffing glue.	= to breathe in, to inhale
supplier	*Lieferant*	person selling or making available sth. that is needed by s.b.	
treatment	*Behandlung*	curing an illness or injury	

vocabulary	dt. Bedeutung	English sentence	syn/opp
(to) withdraw withdrawal	*entziehen* *Entzug*	when s.o. stops doing/ taking sth.	
withdrawal symptoms	*Entzugs-erscheinungen*	the unpleasant feelings that an addict gets when he stops taking a drug/ alcohol/nicotine	
withdrawal treatment	*Entziehungskur*	going on a cure to try to stop taking drugs/alcohol/ nicotine	

3 The court / Law

vocabulary	dt. Bedeutung	English sentence	syn/opp
accusation (to) accuse	*An-, Beschuldigung; Anklage* *beschuldigen*	a statement saying that s.o. has done sth. morally wrong	
(to) acquit acquittal	*freisprechen* *Freispruch*	to declare s.b. to be not guilty of a crime	= to clear s.o.
(to) appeal	*(bei Gericht) Berufung einlegen*	to apply to a superior court for a hearing of the whole or part of a case previously tried in a lower court	
(to) arrest	*festnehmen, verhaften*	to take to the police station	≠ to release
attorney [US]	*Rechtsanwalt*	a lawyer, esp. one qualified to act for clients in a law court	
bail	*Kaution, Bürgschaft*	The defendant was released on bail.	
ban (to) ban	*Verbot* *verbieten*	a formal prohibition	
barrister	*Gerichtsanwalt, Advokat*	a lawyer representing the accused person in court	

vocabulary	dt. Bedeutung	English sentence	syn/opp
capital punish-ment	*Todesstrafe*	Opponents of capital punishment are gaining more support in the USA.	= death penalty
caution	*Vorsicht, Warnung*	Caution! Roadworks ahead.	
charge	*Beschuldigung, Anklage*	He was arrested on charges of burglary and theft.	
client	*Mandant, Klient*	a person who uses the services of a professional person or organisation, e. g. a lawyer	
confession (to) confess	*Geständnis* *gestehen*	The murderer made a full confession to the police.	= admission of guilt ≠ denial
defence counsel	*Verteidiger*	a lawyer engaged in con-ducting cases in court	
defendant	*Angeklagter, Beschuldigter*	The defendant admitted the crime.	
(to) detain	*in Haft behalten*	to keep s.o. in an official place, e. g. a police station	= to keep in custody ≠ to release
detention centre	*Erziehungsanstalt*	an institution for reforming and training young offend-ers	= borstal [UK]
district attorney [US]	*Bezirksanwalt*	a public official who repre-sents a State or the Federal government in court in a particular district	
error of justice	*Justizirrtum*	a wrong judgement or sentence	
evidence	*Beweis*	He was arrested because the police had found enough evidence against him.	= proof

vocabulary	dt. Bedeutung	English sentence	syn/opp
(to) execute	*(ein Urteil) vollstrecken, hinrichten*	to kill s.b. esp. as a legal punishment	
execution	*Hinrichtung*	The execution took place at 5 a.m.	
federal legislation	*Bundesgesetzgebung*	laws imposed by the central government (i. e. in Washington)	
gaol [dʒeil] jail	*Gefängnis*	(old-fashioned for jail) a place where criminals are kept as a punishment	= prison
human rights	*Menschenrechte*	Amnesty International fights for the respect of human rights.	
imprisonment	*Haft-, Gefängnisstrafe*	The accused was sentenced to five years imprisonment.	
indictment	*Anklage*	official accusation of an important person	
inmate	*(Gefängnis-) Insasse, Häftling*	a person in prison or in a hospital for mentally ill people	= prisoner
innocent	*unschuldig*	She claimed that she was absolutely innocent.	
(to) jail	*einsperren*	to put a person behind bars	= to imprison ≠ to release from prison
juror	*der Geschworene*	a member of the jury	
jury	*die Geschworenen*	a group of people in a law court who decide whether the accused person is guilty or not guilty	

vocabulary	dt. Bedeutung	English sentence	syn/opp
juvenile court	*Jugendgericht*	a court that deals with juvenile offenders and children beyond parental control or in need of care	
lawyer	*Rechtsanwalt*	a person trained and qualified in the law who does legal work for other people	
legal process	*Rechtsweg*	action through the processes of the law	
legislation	*Gesetzgebung*	a law or a series of laws	
liability	*Haftung, Haftpflicht*	legal responsibility for sth., especially costs or damages	
litigation	*Prozess, Rechtsstreit*	the process of prosecuting or defending a case in a civil court of law	
oath	*Eid*	a formal promise	
offence	*Vergehen, Verbrechen*	a crime; breaking the law	
offender	*Täter(in), Straffällige(r)*	a person who committed a crime	
penal **penal law**	*Straf-* *Strafrecht*	connected with or relating to punishment	
penalty	*Strafe*	The penalty for parking in the wrong place was increased to $ 50.	
perjury	*Meineid*	the crime of telling lies in court	
(to) plead	*(vor Gericht) plädieren*	The defendant pleaded "not guilty".	
probation **probation officer**	*Bewährung* *Bewährungshelfer*	the system of keeping an official check on s.o. who has broken the law instead of sending him to prison	

vocabulary	dt. Bedeutung	English sentence	syn/opp
prosecution	*strafrechtliche Verfolgung*	the lawyers acting for the state to put the case against a person	
prosecutor	*Ankläger, Anklagevertreter*	a person who conducts legal proceedings in a court of law, esp. on behalf of the public	
provision	*Verordnung, Vorschrift*	a legal statement or paragraph	
(to) release	*freilassen*	After three years he was released from prison.	
(to) sentence	*verurteilen; Urteil*	to give or order a punishment	≠ to set free
solicitor	*Rechtsanwalt*	The young law student started practice in a firm of solicitors.	
(to) sue	*(auf Schadenersatz) verklagen*	to take legal action against s.b. in order to obtain compensation	
suspect	*(Tat-)Verdächtiger*	a person who the police think has committed the crime	
suspicion	*Verdacht*	The policemen's suspicion was aroused when they saw the car drive away at full speed.	
(to) testify	*(vor Gericht) aussagen, bezeugen*	She refused to testify against her husband.	
trial	*Gerichtsverfahren, Prozess*	The defendant is entitled to a fair trial.	= court case
witness	*Zeuge*	a person who appears in a court of law to say what he/she has seen or heard	

Politics

1 Constitution/Political system

vocabulary	dt. Bedeutung	English sentence	syn/opp
amendment (to) amend	*Änderung, Zusatz zur Verfassung* *berichtigen*	The Fifteenth Amendment (1870) to the US Constitution granted the right to vote to African Americans.	
(to) appoint	*ernennen*	The president appoints ambassadors, ministers and consuls.	= to nominate
checks and balances	*gegenseitige Kontrolle und gleichrangige Bedeutung*	The US Constitution established checks and balances between the branches.	
(to) confirm	*bestätigen*	The Senate confirms the president's nominations.	
constitution	*Verfassung*	the law which determines the fundamental political principles of a government	= fundamental law
Constitutional Convention	*verfassungsgebende Versammlung*	The Constitutional Convention took place in Philadelphia in May 1787.	
constitutional monarchy	*konstitutionelle Monarchie*	In a constitutional monarchy the monarch is the head of state but his actions are controlled by the constitution.	
(to) consult	*zurate ziehen*	to get or ask advice from s.b.	
declaration (to) declare	*Erklärung* *verkünden*	a formal announcement	
delegate	*Delegierter, Abgesandter*	a person appointed or elected to represent others	= representative, envoy

vocabulary	dt. Bedeutung	English sentence	syn/opp
deliberately	*absichtlich*	The Constitution is deliberately silent on the question of education.	
(to) derive	*von etw. stammen*	The constitutional guarantee to religious freedom derives from the First Amendment.	= to stem from
(to) nominate nomination	*ernennen* *Ernennung*	The British monarch nominates the prime minister.	= to appoint
regulation	*Vorschrift*	There are no government regulations as to religious services at school.	= ruling, decree
separation of power	*Gewaltenteilung*	The separation of power is a principle of a democratic state.	
succession (to) succeed	*Nachfolge, Erbfolge* *erfolgreich sein; nachfolgen*	a number of people or things that follow each other in time or order	
(to) vest (power)	*(Macht) verleihen*	The Constitution of 1787 vested executive power in a president.	

2 Executive / Government

vocabulary	dt. Bedeutung	English sentence	syn/opp
administration [US] (to) administer	*Regierung; Verwaltung* *verwalten*	the US president and his cabinet who govern the country	
agreement	*Vereinbarung, Vertrag*	The heads of state signed an agreement on economic aid.	

vocabulary	dt. Bedeutung	English sentence	syn/opp
ambassador	*Botschafter*	a diplomat who represents his country in a foreign country	
armed forces	*Streitkräfte*	a country's army, air force and navy	
authority	*Autorität, Vollmacht*	the power or right to give orders or make decisions	
cabinet	*Kabinett*	The presidential cabinet comprises 14 members.	
capacity	*Eigenschaft; Fassungsvermögen*	The prime minister opened the meeting in his capacity as head of the government.	
ceremony	*Feier, Zeremonie*	a formal event	
challenger (to) challenge	*Herausforderer* *herausfordern*	George W. Bush was the Republican challenger of vice-president Al Gore in the presidential election in 2000.	= rival, competitor
commander-in-chief	*Oberbefehlshaber*	The president of the United States is commander-in-chief of the armed forces.	
commission	*Kommission, Ausschuss*	a group of experts who have been chosen to solve a special problem	
(to) comprise	*bestehen aus*	How many counties does Ulster comprise?	= to consist of
consent	*Einwilligung, Zustimmung*	Justices are appointed by the president with the consent of the Senate.	= approval ≠ refusal
coronation	*Krönung*	The coronation of Queen Elizabeth II in 1953 was the first major live TV broadcast in Britain.	

vocabulary	dt. Bedeutung	English sentence	syn/opp
department	*Abteilung, Ministerium*	The presidential cabinet is made up of the heads of the federal departments.	
(to) deploy **deployment**	*(Truppen) verteilen, stationieren* *Stationierung*	The army deployed rockets to protect the country from sudden attacks.	
dictatorship	*Diktatur*	government by a dictator	
(to) dissolve **dissolution**	*auflösen* *Auflösung*	The Queen dissolves parliament on the advice of the prime minister.	
embassy	*Botschaft*	official residence of an ambassador	
emperor	*Kaiser*	the ruler of an empire	
establishment	*Bildung, Gründung, Errichtung*	In 1921 the Irish civil war ended with the establishment of the Irish Free State.	
executive	*ausführende Gewalt*	The president is the head of the executive branch of the federal government.	= government
expenditure	*Ausgabe, Aufwand*	The government increased the defence expenditure.	
(to) exploit **exploitation**	*ausbeuten, ausnutzen* *Ausbeutung*	The native inhabitants were exploited by the white immigrants.	= to take advantage of, to use
extensive	*ausgedehnt, umfassend*	The government offers extensive information on current affairs.	= wide-ranging, far-reaching, detailed
extract	*Auszug*	The document shows an extract from the country's Declaration of Independence.	= excerpt, passage

vocabulary	dt. Bedeutung	English sentence	syn/opp
federal	*Bundes-*	The seat of the federal government of the USA is Washington.	
Foreign Office [BE]	*Außenministerium*	the government department which deals with connections with other countries	= State Department [US]
foreign policy / foreign affairs	*Außenpolitik*	political matters that are connected with other countries	
foreign secretary	*Außenminister*	the head of the Foreign Office	= Secretary of State [US]
head of state	*Staatsoberhaupt*	The US president is head of state and head of the government at the same time.	
Home Office [BE]	*Innenministerium*	the government department which deals with matters inside the country	= Department of the Interior [US]
Home Secretary	*Innenminister*	the head of the Home Office	= Secretary of the Interior [US]
(to) impeach impeachment	*eines Amtes entheben* *Amtsenthebung*	The governor will be impeached for wrongful use of state money.	= to accuse, to put on trial, to prosecute
inaugural address	*Amtsantrittsrede*	Education was the main subject in the president's inaugural address.	
inauguration (to) inaugurate	*Amtseinführung (des US-Präsidenten)* *(feierlich in ein Amt) einführen*	Shortly after Abraham Lincoln's inauguration in 1860, the Civil War broke out.	
incompetent	*unfähig*	Incompetent politicians can cause lots of harm.	= useless ≠ competent

vocabulary	dt. Bedeutung	English sentence	syn/opp
incumbent	*amtierend*	holding a particular post	
(to) instruct	*anweisen*	The officer instructed his men which route to take.	= to direct, to order
involved	*kompliziert*	difficult to understand	= complicated, complex
irrelevant	*unerheblich, belanglos*	beside the point	≠ relevant, important
(to) negotiate negotiation	*verhandeln* *Verhandlung*	The president has the power to negotiate treaties with other nations.	
oath of office	*Amtseid*	Lyndon Johnson took the oath of office on board the presidential jet, Air Force One.	
obsolete	*veraltet*	With the collapse of the Communist threat the original aims of the military alliance became obsolete.	= outmoded, out of date
(to) overthrow	*stürzen, umstürzen*	In 1961 the CIA supported plans to overthrow the Communist government in Cuba.	= to topple
(to) participate participation	*teilnehmen* *Teilnahme*	to take part in an activity	
politics	*Politik*	Well-educated people show a wider interest in politics.	
precaution	*Vorsichts-maßnahme*	sth. done in advance to avoid problems	= safety meas-ure, safeguard
predecessor	*Vorgänger(in)*	a person who had a job or position before s.o. else	≠ successor
presidency	*Präsidentschaft*	the most powerful political position in the United States	
presidential	*Präsidentschafts-, Präsidenten-*	Presidential elections take place every four years.	

vocabulary	dt. Bedeutung	English sentence	syn/opp
prime minister	*Premierminister*	Margaret Thatcher (1979 – 1990) was Britain's first woman prime minister.	
(to) reign	*herrschen*	The Queen reigns, but she does not govern.	
(to) remove **removal**	*entfernen, beseitigen* *Beseitigung*	It is difficult to remove the president from office.	
(to) reside **residence**	*wohnen* *Wohnsitz*	The US president resides in the White House.	
(to) resign **resignation**	*zurücktreten* *Rücktritt*	President Richard M. Nixon resigned in 1974.	
resolution **(to) resolve**	*Entschluss, Entschlossenheit* *etw. lösen, beschließen*	formal statement of opinion	= declaration
royal	*königlich*	Members of the British royal family are always in the news.	
sovereign	*Herrscher; uneingeschränkt, souverän*	a king or queen	
staff	*Personal, Stab*	The president's visit to Dallas was arranged by his White House staff.	
(to) submit **submission**	*etw. vorlegen, unterbreiten* *Vorlage; Unterwerfung*	The new bill will be submitted to parliament for approval.	
summit	*Gipfel*	The president opened the World Summit on Sustainable Development.	
(to) summon	*einberufen*	to call together	

vocabulary	dt. Bedeutung	English sentence	syn/opp
(to) supervise	*überwachen, beaufsichtigen*	Parliament supervises finances and makes laws.	= to control, to oversee, to manage
supervision	*Überwachung*		
term of office	*Amtszeit, Amtsperiode*	The president is elected by the voters for a fixed term of office.	
tyrant	*Diktator*	a person who has complete power in a country and uses it in a cruel and unfair way	= dictator
vice-president	*Vizepräsident, stellvertretender Vorsitzender*	Every four years Americans elect a president and a vice-president.	

3 Legislature / Parliament

vocabulary	dt. Bedeutung	English sentence	syn/opp
(to) adjourn	*(eine Sitzung usw.) vertagen*	to make a pause	= to postpone, to suspend
bill	*Gesetzentwurf*	US Congress approved a bill on lower immigration quotas.	
budget	*Staatshaushalt, Etat*	the financial plan of a country's income from taxes	
chamber	*Kammer*	The House of Lords is the upper chamber of the British legislature.	
committee	*Ausschuss*	A committee will work out suggestions to improve national health care.	
Congress [US]	*Kongress*	The US Congress consists of the Senate and the House of Representatives.	

vocabulary	dt. Bedeutung	English sentence	syn/opp
constitutional	*verfassungsmäßig*	In democratic countries the poor have a constitutional right to welfare.	
(to) determine	*bestimmen, festlegen*	A date for the Queen's state visit to India has yet to be determined.	
(to) empower	*ermächtigen*	to give (s.o.) the official or legal authority to do sth.	= to authorise
(to) enact	*(ein Gesetz) erlassen*	The Belfast Agreement was enacted in November 1998.	
(to) entitle	*berechtigen*	Political refugees are entitled to temporary residence if they can prove that their lives are endangered.	
(to) exceed	*überschreiten*	to be greater than (a number or an amount)	
hereditary	*erblich*	For centuries Europe was largely ruled by hereditary monarchies.	
human rights	*Menschenrechte*	The UN and its family of organizations work to promote respect for human rights.	
issue	*Streitfrage*	an important topic of discussion	= problem
legislation	*Gesetzgebung*	Legislation passed in 1952 allows people of all races to become US citizens.	
legislative legislature	*gesetzgebend* *Gesetzgebung*	Congress makes up the legislative branch of government.	
(to) make a speech	*eine Rede halten*	The Home Secretary will make a speech on the benefits of immigration.	= to deliver a speech

vocabulary	dt. Bedeutung	English sentence	syn/opp
Member of Parliament (MP)	*Parlamentsabgeordneter*	In Britain, a by-election is held when a Member of Parliament dies.	
minutes	*Protokoll*	a summary or record of what is said or decided in parliament	= transcription, record, notes
motion	*parlamentarischer Antrag*	The opposition criticised the government's motion.	= proposal, proposition
(to) nationalise	*verstaatlichen*	to put an industry (steelworks, mines) or a company under the control of the government	≠ to denationalise, to privatise
(to) override	*sich hinwegsetzen über*	to use your authority to reject s.b.'s decision	= to overrule
parliamentary	*parlamentarisch*	The Republic of Ireland is a parliamentary democracy.	
(to) pass a bill	*ein Gesetz verabschieden*	Congress passed a bill which allowed illegal immigrants to stay in the country.	= to adopt ≠ to defeat
policy	*Politik, Taktik*	The government's housing policy came under heavy attack.	= strategy, course of plan
politician	*Politiker*	The Conservative politician Enoch Powell fought against the immigration of foreigners.	
previous	*vorherig, vorhergehend*	coming before; happening or existing before the event s.b. is talking about	= preceding ≠ subsequent
proposition	*Vorschlag, Antrag*	an idea or a plan of action	= proposal, plan, scheme
ratification (to) ratify	*Ratifizierung, Bestätigung* *ratifizieren, bestätigen*	The Equal Rights Amendment was passed by Congress and sent to the states for ratification.	= approval

vocabulary	dt. Bedeutung	English sentence	syn/opp
redundant	*überflüssig; arbeitslos*	not necessary because s.o./sth. else does the same thing	= superfluous, unnecessary
reputation	*Ruf*	Because of hooliganism Britain's reputation has suffered seriously both at home and abroad.	
Senate	*Senat*	The US Senate is composed of 100 senators.	
session	*Sitzung, Sitzungsperiode*	The prime minister opened the session of the European Council in Cardiff.	= meeting, conference
Speaker	*brit. Parlamentspräsident*	The Speaker of the House of Commons chairs meetings and controls discussions.	
(to) suppress **suppression**	*unterdrücken* *Unterdrückung*	Troops were called out to suppress the rebellion.	= to oppress
taxation	*Besteuerung*	collecting money by taxes	
term	*Amtszeit, Sitzungsperiode*	The president is elected by the voters for a fixed term of office.	
Tories	*brit. Konservative*	nickname of the Conservatives in Great Britain	
treaty	*Vertrag*	The Treaty of Maastricht establishing the European Union was signed in 1992.	
violation **(to) violate**	*Verletzung, Bruch* *verletzen*	The cloning of humans is a serious violation of fundamental human rights.	= breach, infringement
wing	*Flügel*	Sinn Fein is the political wing of the Provisional IRA.	

4 Judiciary/Law

vocabulary	dt. Bedeutung	English sentence	syn/opp
(to) balance	*Gleichgewicht herstellen*	The United States is a mix of cultures whose claims must be balanced against each other.	
consent	*Einwilligung, Zustimmung*	The president appoints judges with the consent of the Senate.	≠ refusal, veto, dissent
dissent	*Meinungsverschiedenheit*	For Jefferson, dissent was not only a right but also a necessity.	≠ consent
impartial	*unparteiisch*	not supporting one person or group more than another	= neutral, unbiased ≠ biased
judicial	*gerichtlich*	connected with a court of law, a judge or legal judgement	
judiciary	*Richterstand*	The constitution guarantees the independence of the judiciary.	
justice	*Gerechtigkeit*	the fair treatment of people	≠ injustice
menace	*Bedrohung*	The terrorist menace has spread worldwide.	= threat, peril
(to) nullify nullification	*für nichtig erklären* *Aufhebung*	The 14th amendment of the Constitution of the United States (1868) nullified a decision taken in 1857.	
(to) overturn	*(um)kippen, umdrehen, widerrufen*	In 1954 the Supreme Court overturned the decision taken in 1896.	= to reverse ≠ to endorse
(to) perform	*ausführen, erfüllen*	A free press performs an important function in a democratic society.	

vocabulary	dt. Bedeutung	English sentence	syn/opp
(to) prevail	*die Oberhand gewinnen*	"We will prevail in the war", the president exclaimed.	= to succeed, to triumph ≠ to fail
process	*Prozess, Verfahren, Vorgang*	The peace process has come to a standstill.	
statutory	*gesetzlich*	The system of the presidential elections combines constitutional and statutory requirements.	
Supreme Court [US]	*das Oberste Gericht*	the highest court in the US	
unanimous	*einstimmig*	The court came to a unanimous decision.	
unconstitutional	*verfassungswidrig*	The Supreme Court decided in 1954 that the "separate but equal" concept was unconstitutional.	
void	*null und nichtig*	An unconstitutional law is declared void.	= annulled

5 Elections

vocabulary	dt. Bedeutung	English sentence	syn/opp
ballot	*Wahl; Stimmzettel*	A secret ballot will be held next month.	= vote, election
by-election	*Nachwahl*	Because of the death of the MP for Erith a by-election was necessary.	
campaign	*Wahlkampf*	Most people who run for office limit their campaign to a year or two.	
(to) cast (a vote)	*abstimmen*	Can I cast my vote in writing or by telephone?	

vocabulary	dt. Bedeutung	English sentence	syn/opp
constituency	*Wahlkreis*	In Britain, 650 MPs are elected, one in each constituency.	= electoral district
deposit	*Hinterlegung, Pfand, Kaution*	the amount of money that a candidate in an election to Parliament has to pay, and that is returned if he/she gets enough votes	= security, guarantee
direct representation	*Mehrheitswahl*	Because of the British electoral system of direct representation smaller parties have never played an important role.	
electoral system	*Wahlsystem*	The American electoral system is rather complex.	
electorate	*Wählerschaft*	people who have the right to vote	= voters
eligible (to)	*berechtigt*	At 18 you are eligible to vote.	
FPTP (first-past-the-post)	*Mehrheitswahl*	another word for direct representation; an allusion to horse racing	
general election	*allgemeine Wahl*	In Britain, a general election takes place on a Thursday.	
landslide victory	*überwältigender Wahlsieg*	an election result which has brought an enormous shift from one party to another one	
local elections	*Kommunalwahlen*	The party of the prime minister lost many seats in the latest local elections.	
majority	*Mehrheit*	In order to win a constituency a candidate needs a simple majority of the votes.	≠ minority

vocabulary	dt. Bedeutung	English sentence	syn/opp
majority vote	*Mehrheitswahl*	In Britain, MPs are elected by a majority vote.	
opponent	*Gegner*	The Republican candidate will face his Democratic opponent in three television debates.	= rival, challenger, adversary
overwhelming	*überwältigend*	The new health insurance bill will receive overwhelming support from all parties.	
platform	*Parteiprogramm*	a compilation of the aims of a political party	
poll	*Umfrage, Wahl*	According to the latest poll, Labour will lose many seats in the coming election.	
polling booth	*Wahlkabine*	a small, partly enclosed place in a polling station where people vote secretly	
polling day	*Wahltag*	Polling day in Britain is always a Thursday.	
polling station	*Wahllokal*	a building where people go to vote in an election	
precinct [US]	*Wahlkreis, Wahlbezirk*	a small electoral district of a city or town	
presidential election	*Präsidentschaftswahl*	Waiting for the results of the presidential election in 2000 lasted longer than ever before.	
primaries	*Vorwahlen*	In primaries, party members choose their presidential candidate.	
proportional representation	*Verhältniswahl*	The system of proportional representation gives smaller parties a fairer chance to be represented in parliament.	

vocabulary	dt. Bedeutung	English sentence	syn/opp
representative	*Vertreter*	a person who has been chosen to speak or vote for the interests of a group	
(to) run for (president)	*(für das Amt des Präsidenten) kandidieren*	Very early in his life, John F. Kennedy decided that one day he would run for president.	
splinter party	*Splitterpartei*	a very small party	
turnout	*Wahlbeteiligung*	the number of people who actually vote in an election	
vote	*Abstimmung*	There will be a vote on the government's bill next week.	

From Empire to European Union

1 Empire

vocabulary	dt. Bedeutung	English sentence	syn/opp
acquisition (to) acquire	*Erwerb* *erwerben*	The First British Empire began with the acquisition of territories overseas.	
administration	*Verwaltung*	The colonies were under the administration of the British.	
affairs	*Angelegenheit, Sache*	commercial, professional, public, or personal affairs	
arrogant	*hochmütig*	Very often the British masters behaved in an arrogant way.	= disdainful, haughty, overbearing
benefit	*Vorteil, Nutzen*	Do you think the British rule was also a benefit to the colonised countries?	
(to) colonise	*kolonisieren*	send a group of settlers to (a place) and establish political control over it	
(to) conduct	*geleiten, führen*	British firms conducted their business in the new colonies.	
(to) despise	*verachten, verschmähen*	The native population was often despised by the white masters – and vice versa.	= to look down, to scorn ≠ to appreciate, to esteem
disparity	*Ungleichheit, Unvereinbarkeit*	Energy consumption per head reflects the disparity in the development between industrialised and developing countries.	= disproportion, inequality

vocabulary	dt. Bedeutung	English sentence	syn/opp
diversity	*Vielfalt, Mannigfaltigkeit*	Despite the diversity of its members, the Commonwealth can act globally.	≠ uniformity; identity
Empire	*das britische Weltreich*	The First British Empire began to develop in the 16th century.	
(to) establish	*(Ordnung) schaffen; bilden; gründen*	The British established a new law system in the colonies.	≠ to abolish
(to) exert	*(eine Kraft, einen Einfluss) ausüben*	The new rulers exerted a powerful influence.	= to exercise
exploitation (to) exploit	*Ausnutzung, Ausbeutung* *ausnutzen*	The colonists' primary aim was the exploitation of natural resources.	= to take advantage of, to abuse
(to) extend extension	*verlängern, ausdehnen* *Ausdehnung*	to make or become longer	
heritage	*Erbe*	The problem of immigration grew out of Britain's imperial heritage.	= inheritance
imperial	*kaiserlich; Empire-, des Empires*	George Orwell served in the Imperial Police in British-ruled Burma.	
(to) impose imposition	*(eine Steuer usw.) auferlegen; (eine Geldstrafe) verhängen* *Einführung; Verhängung*	The British parliament imposed a new tax on paper.	
indigenous	*einheimisch*	The indigenous population was regarded as second-class.	= native
manufactured goods	*Industriewaren*	The British used the Empire as a market for their manufactured goods.	

vocabulary	dt. Bedeutung	English sentence	syn/opp
merchant	*Kaufmann*	a buyer and seller of commodities	= trader, businessman
mill	*Fabrik, Textilfabrik*	As a young man David Livingstone worked in a cotton mill in Glasgow.	= factory, works
monopoly	*Monopol*	A protest against the trade monopoly of the East India Company resulted in the Boston Tea Party in 1773.	= trust, syndicate
native	*eingeboren, einheimisch*	The native population was subdued by the colonists.	= indigenous ≠ alien, foreign
(to) neglect	*vernachlässigen*	to give little or no attention	≠ to cherish, to cultivate
outcome	*Ergebnis*	Britain's loss of the North American colonies was the outcome of experience learnt the hard way in 1776.	= result, consequence
persecution **(to) persecute**	*Verfolgung* *verfolgen*	The Pilgrim Fathers were searching for a place to express their faith freely without persecution.	
quest	*Suche*	The quest for new colonies was intensified in the 17th century.	= search
raw materials	*Rohstoffe*	Raw materials from the colonies such as sugar and cotton were manufactured in the factories in England.	
(to) reign	*regieren, herrschen*	to possess or exercise sovereign power	
(to) rule	*regieren*	The British ruled over great parts of the world.	= to govern
ruthless	*unbarmherzig*	The revolt was suppressed with ruthless force.	= merciless

vocabulary	dt. Bedeutung	English sentence	syn/opp
separation (to) separate	*Trennung* *trennen*	The First Empire came to an end with the separation of the American colonies from the British crown in 1783.	
status	*Prestige*	For some people social status is the most important thing in life.	
	Rechtsstellung	The British rejected India's demands for dominion status.	
superiority	*Überlegenheit*	The colonists believed in the superiority of the white race.	≠ inferiority
supremacy	*Vormachtstellung*	the position of being first in influence or power	
trading company	*Handelsgesellschaft*	The trading companies enjoyed many privileges.	
(to) transcend	*über etw. hinausgehen*	to rise above or go beyond the limits	= to surpass, to exceed
unchecked	*unkontrolliert*	Britain's unchecked quest for power is responsible for the exploitation of the colonies.	
undisputed	*unumstritten*	In the 19th century Britain's position in the world was undisputed.	
(to) yield sth. to s.b.	*etw. an jdn. abgeben*	The British failed to yield power to the American colonists.	

2 Commonwealth

vocabulary	dt. Bedeutung	English sentence	syn/opp
(to) acknowledge	*anerkennen*	to recognize the rights, authority, or status of	≠ to ignore, to deny
alliance	*Bündnis*	connection between families, states, parties etc.	= coalition
Commonwealth	*das (britische) Commonwealth*	political organization consisting of nations loyal to the British monarch	
dominion	*Herrschaftsgebiet, brit. Dominion (selbstständiges Land des Commonwealth)*	The British gave Canada dominion status in 1867.	
(to) emerge	*entstehen, hervorgehen*	The multiracial Commonwealth began to emerge after the First World War.	
independence movement	*Unabhängigkeits bewegung*	Gandhi became the key figure in the independence movement in India.	
independent	*unabhängig*	free from control by others	= free, autonomous, sovereign
interior	*intern, innere, Innen-*	Britain's former colonies were granted home rule to decide about their interior affairs themselves.	
loose	*lose*	The Commonwealth is a loose association of about 50 states.	
membership	*Mitgliedschaft*	In 1949, India decided to continue its membership in the Commonwealth.	
privilege	*Vorrecht, Privileg*	a right granted as a peculiar advantage or favour	

vocabulary	dt. Bedeutung	English sentence	syn/opp
selfish	*selbstsüchtig*	The Commonwealth is not a selfish organisation.	= egoistic, self-interested
sovereign	*souverän, uneingeschränkt*	The Commonwealth includes more than fifty sovereign nations and several dependencies.	= autonomous, independent
(to) transform	*etw./jdn. verwandeln*	The British transformed their Empire into the Commonwealth of nations.	= to change, to convert
voluntary	*freiwillig*	The Commonwealth is a voluntary association of independent states.	≠ involuntary, obligatory

3 European Union

vocabulary	dt. Bedeutung	English sentence	syn/opp
(to) abolish abolition	*abschaffen, aufheben* *Abschaffung*	to bring to an end/to put an end to sth.	= to remove, to do away with
(to) achieve achievement	*erlangen, erreichen* *Vollbringung (große Tat)*	It seems extremely difficult to achieve an agreement on a common agricultural policy.	= to attain
(to) admit admittance, admission	*zulassen, etw. zugeben* *Einlass, Eintritt, Zutritt*	The UK, Denmark and Ireland were admitted to the European Economic Community in 1973.	≠ to exclude
(to) adopt	*annehmen*	Other EU countries might adopt the euro soon.	
agriculture	*Landwirtschaft*	Agriculture is a very difficult field in EU politics.	
(to) apply (for) application	*sich bewerben um* *Bewerbung*	Britain first applied for membership in 1963 – but was not admitted.	

vocabulary	dt. Bedeutung	English sentence	syn/opp
bailout	*Rettungsaktion*	To cope with the financial crisis several European banks had to ask the governments for a bailout.	= (financial) rescue
(to) cease	*aufhören*	By 1980, the EEC had ceased to develop further.	≠ to stop, to discontinue
civil servant	*Beamter*	A civil servant is a person who works for the government.	
(to) commit commitment	*sich verpflichten* *Verpflichtung*	In the treaties the member states also committed themselves to improve the effectiveness of a Common Foreign and Security Policy (CFSP).	
community	*Gemeinschaft*	The new members added significantly to the size of the community.	
competition (to) compete	*Wettbewerb, Konkurrenz* *konkurrieren*	Many managers thought that more competition would cause higher unemployment.	
confederation	*Bündnis*	an organization which consists of a number of parties or groups	= alliance
Council of Ministers	*Ministerrat*	The French finance minister Jacques Delors submitted to the Council of Ministers the idea to create a single market.	
counterweight	*Gegengewicht*	The EU was created as a counterweight to the large consumer markets in Japan and the USA.	= counter-balance

vocabulary	dt. Bedeutung	English sentence	syn/opp
dilemma	*Zwangslage*	a situation in which a difficult choice has to be made between two or more bad alternatives	= predicament
economic policy	*Wirtschaftspolitik*	The total number of new jobs would be higher if the government pursued a better economic policy.	
efficiency	*Leistungsfähigkeit*	The governments must improve the efficiency of the EU.	= effectiveness, performance
EC (European Community)	*EG (Europäische Gemeinschaft)*	name of the European Union between 1973 and 1993	
EEC (European Economic Community)	*EWG (Europäische Wirtschaftsgemeinschaft)*	name of the original alliance of six European countries begun in 1957	
emergency measure	*Notmaßnahme*	The EU took emergency measures to protect the value of the euro.	
enlargement	*Vergrößerung*	The representatives of the EU discussed the enlargement of the union.	= extension
EU (European Union)	*EU (Europäische Union)*	The Treaty of Maastricht (1993) marks the beginning of the EU.	
(to) evolve	*(sich weiter-) entwickeln*	to develop gradually	
evolution	*Entwicklung*		
improvement	*Verbesserung, Fortschritt*	Many welcomed the improvements in the free movement of people.	
influential	*einflussreich*	The plan of extending the EU was strongly supported by influential managers.	

vocabulary	dt. Bedeutung	English sentence	syn/opp
(to) intend	*beabsichtigen*	The member countries intended to agree on a common defence policy.	= to plan
isolation (to) isolate	*Absonderung, Trennung* *trennen*	without relation to other people or things	
merger	*Fusion, Zusammenlegung*	A merger of two companies often results in a loss of jobs.	= amalgamation, union
monetary	*Währungs-*	In 2002, the euro became the monetary unit of 12 European countries.	
(to) predict prediction	*voraussagen* *Voraussage, Vorhersage*	Experts predict that there will be a significant loss of jobs in the industrialised countries.	= to forecast
presidency	*Präsidentschaft*	Each EU member state takes over the presidency for six months.	
prospect	*Aussicht*	Business managers welcomed the prospect of increased trade.	= outlook, perspective
(to) pursue pursuit pursuance	*verfolgen, betreiben* *Verfolgung*	The government pursues a strict financial policy.	= to follow
quota	*(Einfuhr-) Kontingent*	The EEC countries did away with all quotas between the member countries.	
referendum	*Volksentscheid*	In 1975, Britain's membership to the EC was approved by the population in the first national referendum in British history.	
(to) sign	*unterzeichnen*	The Treaty of Rome was signed in March 1957.	

vocabulary	dt. Bedeutung	English sentence	syn/opp
significant	*deutlich, merklich*	Ireland profited significantly from its membership in the community.	= considerable, substantial
single currency	*Binnenwährung*	The single currency has made it easier to compare prices in Europe.	
single market	*Binnenmarkt*	Jacques Delors developed the plan for the creation of a single market.	
stimulus	*Reiz, Ansporn*	The preparation of the single currency provided the stimulus to cut inflation.	= incentive
(to) submit	*unterbreiten, vorlegen*	The Council of Ministers will submit a new proposal to increase the number of members.	
survey	*Untersuchung, Umfrage*	A survey shows a high degree of scepticism against more EU regulations.	= study, analysis
target	*Ziel*	In the Treaty of Rome of 1957, the founding countries set themselves a clear target.	= aim, objective
tariffs [Pl.]	*Zolltarife, Zölle*	The EEC countries reduced tariffs between member countries.	
treaty	*(Staats-)Vertrag*	Six countries (France, Italy, Belgium, Germany, Luxembourg and the Netherlands) signed the Treaty of Rome in 1957.	= agreement, convention
turning point	*Wende, Wendepunkt*	The Treaty of Maastricht (1993) was a turning point in the development of the EU.	

World affairs

1 War and peace

vocabulary	dt. Bedeutung	English sentence	syn/opp
(to) advance	*vorrücken, vordringen*	The general's army managed to advance even further.	= to move forward ≠ to recede
(to) advocate	*verteidigen, befürworten*	The Prime Minister seems to advocate a reduction of defence costs.	= to support, to back
(to) affect	*beeinträchtigen, schädigen, angreifen*	The relationship between the two countries was affected by the discussion on human rights.	
alliance	*Bündnis*	An alliance is a relationship in which two or more people or groups work together for some purpose.	= coalition
ally	*Verbündeter, Alliierter*	The USA and its European allies met for discussions in Brussels.	
armament	*Aufrüstung, Rüstung*	We talk of armament when a country increases the number of its weapons.	
armistice	*Waffenstillstand*	An armistice is an agreement between two countries at war with one another to stop the fighting.	= truce
armour	*Rüstung*	defensive covering for the body; often made of metal	
arms	*Waffen*	One can hardly think of more destructive weapons than nuclear arms.	= weapons

vocabulary	dt. Bedeutung	English sentence	syn/opp
arms control	*Rüstungskontrolle*	The two superpowers agreed to introduce mutual arms control.	
arms race	*Wettrüsten, Rüstungswettlauf*	Because of the arms race a lot of money is wasted.	
(to) assign	*bestimmen, (Aufgabe) zuweisen*	The government assigned the army to control the streets at night.	
balance of power	*Machtgleichgewicht*	During the Cold War people thought that only a balance of power could guarantee peace in Europe.	
(to) betray	*verraten*	to reveal to an enemy important information	
bloodshed	*Blutvergießen*	There was no evidence of bloodshed or attack.	
casualties	*Verluste*	No casualties were reported.	= victims, losses
(to) compensate (for)	*entschädigen*	The army has to compensate farmers for damage done to their land during manoeuvres.	= to repay
conscientious objector	*Wehrdienstverweigerer*	In Austria, conscientious objectors have to do community service instead of military service.	
conscript	*Wehrpflichtiger*	A conscript usually serves the army more unwillingly than a volunteer or professional.	
cowardice	*Feigheit*	He despised them for their cowardice and ignorance.	≠ courage
(to) cut	*(Kosten) kürzen*	It is the government's intention to cut defence costs.	= to reduce, to trim

vocabulary	dt. Bedeutung	English sentence	syn/opp
(to) declare war	*Krieg erklären*	The Japanese declared war on the USA after the attack on Pearl Harbor in December 1941.	
defence expenditure	*Verteidigungsausgaben*	Most governments have reduced their defence expenditure.	
(to) defy	*sich auflehnen, widersetzen*	The officer defied the order of the commanding general.	= to resist
depressing	*deprimierend*	The TV picture of the terrible war had a depressing effect on the viewers.	= gloomy, sad, discouraging
detente	*Entspannung*	In the 1970s and 80s, detente created a live and let live attitude in Europe.	
deterrent	*Abschreckung*	Some people think nuclear weapons are the best deterrent against war.	
disarmament	*Abrüstung*	a process in which countries agree to reduce the number of weapons they have	
dissolution (to) dissolve	*Auflösung* *auflösen*	The defeated army fled in dissolution.	
gloomy	*trostlos*	Pessimists expect a gloomy future as far as social peace is concerned.	= dark, sad, pessimistic
human rights	*Menschenrechte*	The president asked all countries to respect human rights (such as life, liberty and the pursuit of happiness).	
invincible	*unbesiegbar*	too powerful to be conquered or defeated	

vocabulary	dt. Bedeutung	English sentence	syn/opp
martial law	*Kriegs-, Standrecht*	The country has now spent more than eight years under martial law.	
mercenary	*Söldner*	a soldier hired into foreign service	
national service	*Wehrdienst*	Compulsory national service was abolished in Germany in 2011.	= military service, conscription
nuclear disarmament	*atomare Abrüstung*	Nuclear disarmament on a world-wide scale was of vital importance in the 1980s.	≠ atomic war
nuclear war	*Atomkrieg*	If a nuclear war broke out, it would mean the end of the world as we know it.	= atomic war
nuclear weapons	*Atomwaffen*	All nuclear weapons should be banned and destroyed.	= atomic arms
obedience (to) obey	*Gehorsam* *gehorchen, folgen*	Unquestioning obedience is necessary for an army to function.	
(to) outnumber	*an Zahl überlegen sein, übertreffen*	In this group the men outnumber the women by four to one.	
policy of detente	*Entspannungspolitik*	The president's policy of detente led to an agreement with the USSR.	
professional armed forces	*Berufsstreitkräfte*	Britain has had professional armed forces since 1960.	
raid	*(überraschender) Angriff*	Thousands were killed in the air-raid.	
(to) ravage	*schänden, vergewaltigen*	Public buildings were ravaged by looters and plunderers.	= to devastate

vocabulary	dt. Bedeutung	English sentence	syn/opp
refugee	*Flüchtling*	As a result of the Second World War millions of refugees were driven from their homes in Europe.	
reinforcement	*Verstärkung*	As a matter of reinforcement the government sent more troops to Belfast.	
(to) retreat	*sich zurückziehen*	After losing the first battle, the army had to retreat.	= to withdraw
shelter	*Schutz(raum)*	During the Second World War thousands of Londoners sought shelter in underground stations.	
shortage	*Knappheit*	Wars have always been accompanied by a shortage of food and water.	≠ surplus
(to) smash	*zerschmettern, zerschlagen*	During the revolt people were injured, cars burned and property was smashed.	= to break, to shatter, to destroy
(to) spill blood	*Blut vergießen*	The blood of innocent people was spilled in Northern Ireland.	
stronghold	*Hochburg, Stützpunkt*	Wales remained a Celtic stronghold till the end of the 13th century.	
(to) summon	*zusammenrufen, einberufen*	to demand or request the presence or service of s.o.	
supply	*Nachschub*	The armed forces waited for the supply sent out on ferryboats.	
surrender	*Kapitulation, Übergabe, Aufgabe*	They tried to starve us into surrender.	= capitulation

vocabulary	dt. Bedeutung	English sentence	syn/opp
traitor	*Verräter*	s.o. who is not loyal to his country or to a group to which he belongs	
unconditional	*bedingungslos*	In 1945, the allies demanded the unconditional surrender of the German army.	
unrelenting	*unerbittlich*	Members of the rifle association try to explain their unrelenting opposition to gun control.	
valour	*Heldenmut*	strength of mind or spirit that enables a person to cope with a dangerous situation	≠ cowardliness, fear
(to) vanquish	*besiegen, überwinden*	They managed to vanquish all their enemies.	= to conquer, to defeat, to overcome
vengeance	*Vergeltung, Rache*	The partisans vowed to take vengeance on the occupying forces.	
volunteer	*Freiwilliger*	"One volunteer is better than ten conscripts."	
warfare	*Kriegsführung*	Atomic warfare must be avoided at all costs.	
warrior	*Krieger*	This book is about the noble king, his bravest warrior and the greatest battles.	= fighter, combatant
(to) withdraw	*(sich) zurückziehen*	The British had to withdraw their troops from all the countries east of Suez.	= to retreat
wound [u:]	*Wunde*	an injury to the body from violence or an accident	

2 Northern Ireland

vocabulary	dt. Bedeutung	English sentence	syn/opp
animosity	*Abneigung*	a deep-rooted feeling of dislike	= hostility, enmity ≠ liking
(to) assert	*auf etw. bestehen, einfordern*	Militant groups asserted their right to keep weapons.	= to affirm, to declare
atrocity	*Gräueltat*	(an act of) great evil, esp. cruelty	
bigot	*Eiferer*	s.o. with unreasonable ideas about politics, religion or race who will not accept the opinions of anyone who disagrees	= fanatic, maniac
bloodshed	*Blutvergießen*	The Irish conflict caused massive bloodshed and misery.	
(to) boast	*prahlen*	to exaggerate one's abilities	= to brag
boundary	*Grenze*	a line which marks the limits of an area	
ceasefire	*Feuerpause*	an agreement to stop fighting	
ceaseless	*endlos*	without stopping	= unending, continuous
civil war	*Bürgerkrieg*	The Irish civil war led to the partition of the island in 1920.	
commemoration	*Gedenken*	Protestant Unionists march through Catholic areas in commemoration of the Battle of the Boyne in 1690.	
compromise	*Kompromiss*	settlement of differences by mutual concessions	

vocabulary	dt. Bedeutung	English sentence	syn/opp
(to) conclude	*(eine Vereinbarung) schließen*	The Good Friday Agreement was concluded on April 10, 1998.	
(to) condemn	*verurteilen, verdammen*	to say that sth. is completely unacceptable	
(to) condone	*(stillschweigend) dulden*	to tolerate or allow sth. which is morally wrong to continue	
(to) confine	*beschränken*	Terrorist acts were not confined to members of the IRA.	= to restrict
cover name	*Deckname*	a name concealing the true identity of a person	
credibility	*Glaubwürdigkeit*	combination of respect and trust	
deadline	*letzter Termin*	a date or time before which sth. must be done or completed	
(to) decommission	*stilllegen, abgeben, ausmustern*	to hand over arms to the authorities	
(to) deny	*abstreiten*	to state that sth. is not true	≠ to acknowledge, to admit
(to) deploy deployment	*(Truppen) einsetzen* *Aufmarsch*	The British deployed troops to avoid a civil war.	
descendant (to) descend	*Nachkomme* *herabgehen*	The descendants of the Presbyterian settlers have ruled the province for centuries.	≠ ancestor, forebear, forefather
(to) deteriorate deterioration	*sich verschlechtern* *Verschlechterung*	Relations between the opposing groups have deteriorated sharply.	= to become worse

vocabulary	dt. Bedeutung	English sentence	syn/opp
direct rule	*Verwaltung Nordirlands durch die britische Regierung*	Direct rule by the British began in 1972.	
(to) disarm	*abrüsten, entwaffnen*	An important point in the agreement was that terrorists would disarm.	
disarmament	*Entwaffnung*		
dominant	*vorherrschend, tonangebend*	Protestants in Ulster have always held a dominant position.	= superior, leading
DUP (Democratic Unionist Party)		party which represents unionist interests	
durable	*dauerhaft*	Can a durable peace be achieved?	= lasting, permanent, stable ≠ fragile, weak
Eire	*Irland*	the Gaelic name for Ireland, the official name of the Republic of Ireland from 1937 to 1949	
(to) emerge	*herauskommen, auftauchen*	It is hoped that a compromise will emerge from the talks between the rival parties.	= to come out of ≠ to disappear, to dissolve
(to) erupt	*ausbrechen*	Violence erupted at the beginning of the 1970s.	= to break out
(to) exceed	*übersteigen, überschreiten*	The number of killings in Northern Ireland on both sides exceeded 3,600.	= surpass
fragile	*zerbrechlich, brüchig, unsicher*	Any agreement in Ulster is rather fragile.	= delicate, frail ≠ tough
gloom	*Hoffnungslosigkeit*	almost complete darkness	= sadness

vocabulary	dt. Bedeutung	English sentence	syn/opp
Good Friday Agreement	*Karfreitags-abkommen*	On Good Friday 1998, all parties involved in the Northern Ireland conflict signed an agreement that peace in the province can only be achieved without violence.	
grievance	*Beschwerde, Klage*	to complain or protest about sth.	
(to) harass	*schikanieren*	to put pressure on s.o., even to attack s.o.	= to annoy, to pester
home rule	*Selbstverwaltung*	The campaign for Irish home rule began in the late 19th century.	
Home Rule Act	*Gesetz zur politischen Selbstverwaltung Nordirlands*	The Home Rule Act was passed in 1914.	
incessant	*ununterbrochen*	sth. going on without interruption	= ceaseless, constant ≠ intermittent
incitement	*Anstiftung, Aufwiegelung*	incitement of racial hatred	= encouragement ≠ restraint
incompatible	*unvereinbar*	Political observers think that the views of the Protestants and the Catholics are incompatible.	= conflicting, discrepant ≠ compatible
inevitable	*unvermeidlich*	Political leaders see the confrontation in Ulster as an inevitable clash of civilizations and religions.	≠ avoidable
(to) inflict	*jdm. etw. zufügen*	Irish Catholics fight against the injustices inflicted upon the people of Ireland.	

vocabulary	dt. Bedeutung	English sentence	syn/opp
(to) infuriate	*jdn. wütend machen*	to make s.o. angry	
(to) intimidate	*einschüchtern*	to put fear into s.o.	= to frighten
IRA (Provisional IRA)	*Irisch-Republikanische Armee*	illegal terrorist organisation whose aim is to drive out the British soldiers and to achieve reunification of Northern Ireland and the Republic	
irreconcilable	*unvereinbar, unversöhnlich*	The political views of the Protestants and the Catholics in Ulster are irreconcilable.	= incompatible
issue	*Streitfrage, Problem*	a problem or a political decision	
loyalist	*Befürworter der politischen Union zwischen GB und Nordirland*	in Ulster: the Protestants; they are seen as loyal to Britain	
(to) maintain	*aufrechterhalten; behaupten*	Troops were sent in to maintain public order.	= to keep up, to preserve, to sustain
mischief	*Unfug*	behaviour that causes trouble and possibly damage	
mutual	*gegenseitig, beiderseitig*	The Good Friday Agreement has not turned mutual dislike into cooperation.	
(to) negotiate	*verhandeln*	to try to reach an agreement by talking with the other party	
(to) partition	*(ein Land) teilen*	to divide into two or more parts	

vocabulary	dt. Bedeutung	English sentence	syn/opp
perfidious	*heimtückisch, gemein*	Perfidious acts of violence will not improve the prospects for peace.	= disloyal; dishonest, treacherous
Plantation	*Kolonisierung, Besiedlung*	Plantation of Ulster: settlement of Scots and Englishmen	
predominance	*Vorherrschaft, Überlegenheit*	Ulster has long been an area of Protestant predominance.	
prejudice	*Vorurteil*	having an unreasonable or unfair idea about s.b. or sth.	= bias
(to) preserve	*erhalten, bewahren*	Everything must be done to preserve the peace in Ulster.	= to conserve, to keep up
Provos (Provisionals)	*Angehörige der IRA*	members of the Provisional Irish Republican Army (IRA)	
reconciliation (to) reconcile	*Versöhnung, Aussöhnung* *versöhnen*	There are still hopes for reconciliation between Roman Catholics and Protestants.	
remedy	*Heilmittel, Lösung*	a way of curing sth.	= cure
repentance	*Reue*	the state of being sorry for the wrong one has done	= remorse
resentment	*Verbitterung*	the feeling of not liking sth.; the feeling that one has been badly treated	= antipathy, animosity
(to) retain	*behalten*	Protestant loyalists are determined to retain the constitutional link with London.	= to keep, to continue

vocabulary	dt. Bedeutung	English sentence	syn/opp
reunification **(to) reunify**	*Wiedervereinigung* *wiedervereinigen*	The reunification of the whole island is an important element of the Irish constitution.	
sectarian	*konfessionell bedingt, sektiererisch*	Provos are responsible for a large number of sectarian killings.	
sectarianism	*Sektierertum*	strong, even violent support of a particular religious denomination and its political representation	
settlement	*Einigung*	Further efforts were made to achieve a political settlement.	= agreement
Sinn Fein	*Sinn Fein (Irish Gaelic: "we ourselves")*	the political party representing Catholics in Northern Ireland	
Ulster	*Nordirland*	Ulster is the northern province of Ireland; six of its nine counties belong to the United Kingdom.	
Ulster Unionists	*nordirische Unionisten*	Protestants who are in favour of the union of Northern Ireland and Great Britain	
UUP (Ulster Unionist Party)	*Protestantenpartei Nordirlands (probritische Partei)*	party in Northern Ireland which represents unionist interests	

Economy

1 Economic policy

vocabulary	dt. Bedeutung	English sentence	syn/opp
affluent	*wohlhabend, reich*	affluent people are very rich and have a high standard of living	= rich, wealthy, prosperous
(to) balance	*ausgleichen, bilanzieren*	to equal or equalize in weight, number, or proportion	
balance of payments	*Zahlungsbilanz*	The British balance of payments shows a surplus.	
black economy	*Schattenwirtschaft*	work which is not official but which people do to avoid paying taxes	= twilight economy, hidden economy
boom	*Hochkonjunktur*	period of economic prosperity	
budget	*Etat, öffentlicher Haushalt*	The government tries to balance the budget.	
commerce	*Handel, Verkehr*	Commerce between England and the USA has grown steadily.	= business, trade
commodity	*Ware*	a raw material or primary agricultural product that can be bought and sold, such as copper or coffee	
depression	*Wirtschaftskrise*	a long and severe recession in an economy (the Great Depression of 1929)	≠ boom
free enterprise	*freies Unternehmertum*	an economic system in which private business operates without interference of the state	

vocabulary	dt. Bedeutung	English sentence	syn/opp
globalisation	*Globalisierung*	a worldwide market without any barriers with free flow of capital, products and services	
gross domestic product (GNP)	*Bruttoinlandsprodukt*	the total value of goods produced and services provided by a country during one year	
magnitude	*Größe, Ausmaß*	The Great Depression in the 1930s was of a much greater magnitude than any other business downturn.	= size, scope, extent, dimension
monetary	*Geld-, Währungs-*	One of the aims of the Bank of England's monetary policy is to keep inflation low.	
(to) nationalise	*verstaatlichen*	to transfer (a major branch of industry or commerce) from private to state ownership or control, e. g. railways	≠ to privatise
plentiful	*reichlich*	The successes of American business and industry are based on plentiful resources, the geographical size of the country and its population.	≠ scarce
purchasing power	*Kaufkraft*	Different currencies have different purchasing power both in international trade and at home.	
recession	*Rezession, Konjunkturrückgang*	a period, shorter than a depression, during which there is a decline in economic trade and prosperity	= slump, stagnation

vocabulary	dt. Bedeutung	English sentence	syn/opp
service industry	*Dienstleistungs-sektor*	More jobs will be created in the service industry.	
schedule	*Zeit-/Fahrplan*	The assistant worked out a schedule for the manager's trip to Japan.	= timetable, programme, plan
supply and demand	*Angebot und Nachfrage*	Supply and demand determine the price of a product.	
tight	*streng; dicht*	The government followed a tight monetary policy to control inflation.	= strict, tough, hard
virtually	*praktisch, eigentlich*	Virtually all the net growth in employment in recent years has come from part-time jobs.	= practically, nearly

2 The world of work

vocabulary	dt. Bedeutung	English sentence	syn/opp
accountant	*Steuerberater(in), Wirtschafts-prüfer(in)*	a person who keeps or inspects the financial accounts of a company	
alienation	*Entfremdung*	Many workers who have to carry out boring routine work suffer from job alienation.	
apprentice	*Lehrling, Auszu-bildender*	If you want to learn a trade properly you must start as an apprentice.	
apprenticeship	*Lehrzeit, Lehre*		
(to) assemble	*montieren, zu-sammensetzen*	In that huge building over there they assemble the latest model of the Airbus.	= to put together, to build
blue-collar worker	*Arbeiter(in)*	worker who wears (mostly) blue work clothes or protective clothing	≠ white-collar worker

vocabulary	dt. Bedeutung	English sentence	syn/opp
board of directors	*Verwaltungsrat, Aufsichtsrat*	The members of the board of directors will meet the trade union representatives on Monday.	= supervisory board, administrative board
careers officer	*Berufsberater*	A careers officer came to the school to inform school-leavers about their job prospects.	
CEO (chief executive officer)	*Generaldirektor, Geschäftsführer*	person responsible for a firm's business transactions	
commission	*Provision*	money paid to an agent or employee for performing a service	
consultant	*Berater(in)*	a person who provides expert advice	
conveyor belt	*Montageband, Fließband*	Tom Birch stands at a conveyor belt all day.	= assembly line
craftsman craftsmanship	*(gelernter) Handwerker* *Kunstfertigkeit*	Mr Tylor is an excellent craftsman: he really knows how to make beautiful chairs.	
deduction (to) deduct	*Abzug* *abziehen*	an amount taken away from a sum of money	≠ addition
(to) dismiss	*entlassen*	I cannot believe that the factory wants to dismiss more than 500 people from their jobs!	= to discharge, to sack, to fire
dole (to) be on the dole	*Arbeitslosengeld* *Arbeitslosengeld bekommen, stempeln gehen*	Fred Compton has been on the dole for over eight months.	
employee	*Arbeitnehmer, Angestellter*	This company has more than 4,600 employees.	

vocabulary	dt. Bedeutung	English sentence	syn/opp
employer	*Arbeitgeber*	The central organisation of British employers is called Confederation of British Industry.	
(to) found	*gründen*	IBM (International Business Machines Corporation) was founded in 1911.	= to establish, to start, to set up
freelancer	*Freiberufler(in)*	a person who works without a long-term commitment to any one employer	
friendly takeover	*freundliche Übernahme*	when a company buys another firm with the approval of that firm	≠ hostile takeover
hostile takeover	*feindliche Übernahme*	when a company buys another firm against the expressed wishes of that firm	≠ friendly takeover
human resources	*Arbeitskräfte*	the personnel of a business or organization	= staff
Inland Revenue [UK]	*Finanzamt*	the department responsible for the collection of taxes	= finance authority
job centre	*Arbeitsamt*	Every morning there is a long queue of job seekers outside the job centre.	= labor office [US], labour exchange
labour	*Arbeit, Arbeitskräfte*	unskilled labour	
labour exchange	*Arbeitsamt*	Every morning Gerry goes down to the labour exchange to find out if there are any suitable jobs going.	= job centre, labor office [US]
lay-off	*vorübergehende Entlassung*	Many managers feared that increased competition would cause lay-offs.	
(to) lay s.b. off	*jdn. entlassen*	When the new robot was installed twenty workers were laid off.	

vocabulary	dt. Bedeutung	English sentence	syn/opp
limited company (ltd)	*Gesellschaft mit beschränkter Haftung (GmbH)*	London's renowned department store Harrods Ltd. was founded as a grocery store in 1849.	
(to be) listed on the stock exchange	*an der Börse notiert sein*	Since November 1998 DaimlerChrysler shares are listed on the stock exchange in New York.	
livelihood	*Auskommen, Lebensunterhalt, Unterhalt*	Pamela Whitby earns her livelihood by teaching.	= living
(to) make a living	*seinen Lebensunterhalt verdienen*	to earn money to live on	
management buy-out (MBO)	*Ankauf eines Unternehmens durch Mitglieder der Firma*	The company was only able to stay in business after an MBO.	
manpower [Pl.]	*Arbeitskräfte*	As the new product sold rather well, the firm decided to increase manpower in the production plant.	= workers, labour force
manufactured goods	*Fertigwaren*	More money is earned by the sale of manufactured goods than with the sale of primary products.	= finished products
merger (to) merge	*Fusion* *fusionieren*	The merger of Chrysler Corporation and Daimler-Benz was completed in 1998.	
national insurance contributions	*Beiträge zur Sozialversicherung*	National insurance contributions have gone up by 1.5 %.	= social security contributions
notice (to) give notice	*Kündigung* *kündigen*	In order to save costs the firm had to give notice to 250 employees.	

vocabulary	dt. Bedeutung	English sentence	syn/opp
without notice	*fristlos*	As he had stolen some tools from the shop floor, Angus McDowell was dismissed without notice.	
overtime	*Überstunden*	time worked over and above one's normal working hours	
parent company	*Muttergesellschaft*	The new firm already accounts for 15 % of its parent company's income.	
personnel	*Personal, Belegschaft*	There are rumours about a slight reduction of the personnel in the Hendon branch office.	= staff, workforce
plant	*Anlage, Werk*	German firms helped to build a chemical plant in Libya.	= works, factory, mill
profession (to) enter a profession	*(akademischer) Beruf* *einen Beruf ergreifen*	For a profession (e. g. lawyer, doctor, teacher) an advanced education and a special training are required.	
(to) promote promotion	*jdn. befördern* *Beförderung*	The board of directors has decided to promote Alwyn Reeves to deputy staff manager.	
public limited company (plc)	*Aktiengesellschaft (AG)*	Pearson plc, a multinational publishing and education company, has its headquarters in London.	= corporation [US]
(to) qualify	*sich eignen*	In order to qualify for the job, you will need more experience.	= be suited for
(to) recruit	*jdn. einstellen*	to enrol s.b. as a worker; to take on people as workers	= to enrol, to hire

vocabulary	dt. Bedeutung	English sentence	syn/opp
redundancy payment	*Abfindung*	Most employees who lost their jobs received redundancy payments.	
requirement	*Anforderung, Voraussetzung*	The most important job requirements include ability to work in a team, flexibility and experience.	
revenue	*Einkünfte*	the total income	
(to) retire	*in Pension gehen, in Rente gehen, sich pensionieren lassen*	Harry can hardly wait till he's 62, because then he wants to retire and work in his garden all day long.	
royalties	*Tantiemen*	the sum of money which is paid e. g. to an author	
sack (to) sack	*Rausschmiss, Entlassung* *rausschmeißen*	The manager was sick and tired of Brian being late almost every day, so he gave him the sack.	
salary	*Gehalt*	If you take this job, you can earn a salary of £ 24,900 a year.	
sales rep(resentative)	*Vertreter(in)*	a person who travels around selling his company's goods	
self-employed	*selbstständig*	earning/income directly from one's own business	
semiskilled (worker)	*angelernt(er Arbeiter/Arbeitnehmer)*	a person who has less training in a job than a skilled labourer	
senior manager	*leitende(r) Angestellte(r)*	a manager holding a higher and more important position in a company	
share	*Aktie*	After the crash at the stock exchange people hesitated to buy shares again.	

vocabulary	dt. Bedeutung	English sentence	syn/opp
shareholder	*Aktionär*	s.o. who owns a share in property or in a company	
shift	*Schicht*	For most of his life William Peel has been working night shift.	
skilled	*ausgebildet, Fach-*	a fully qualified worker	
skilled worker	*Facharbeiter*	A skilled worker has greater chances of finding the type of job he wants.	
skill shortage	*Facharbeitermangel*	shortage of trained and experienced staff	
staff	*Belegschaft*	The company employs a staff of 287.	= workforce
staff manager	*Personalchef*	I'd like to talk to the staff manager about my complaint, please.	= manager of personnel, HR manager
state-owned company	*Staatsunternehmen*	a company in the hands and under control of the state	
stocks	*Aktien, Wertpapiere*	capital of a company, usually divided into shares	
subsidiary	*Tochter(unternehmen)*	a firm controlled by a holding company	
(to) subsidize	*subventionieren, bezuschussen*	In developing countries governments subsidize basic foods.	
supplier	*Lieferant*	a person selling or making available sth. that is needed	
trade	*Gewerbe, Branche*	occupation; area of business or industry	
trainee	*Praktikant, in der Ausbildung Stehender*	Richard works as a trainee reporter for 'The Daily Telegraph'.	

vocabulary	dt. Bedeutung	English sentence	syn/opp
unemployed	*arbeitslos*	Ralph has been unemployed for two years.	= jobless, out of work
unemployment benefit (to) draw ~	*Arbeitslosengeld* *(Arbeitslosen-) Unterstützung beziehen*	As Jennifer has lost her job, she now draws unemployment benefit.	= unemployment funds
unskilled (worker)	*ungelernt(er Arbeiter/Arbeitnehmer)*	s.b. who has no training	≠ skilled
upheaval	*Umwälzung; Aufruhr*	The Industrial Revolution caused a great upheaval in England's social structure.	= upturn
vacancy	*freie Stelle, offene Stelle*	Martin, who's a trained carpenter, is looking for a vacancy in his area.	= job
wage	*Lohn, Arbeitslohn*	a weekly payment for work	= pay, earnings
white-collar worker	*(Büro-)Angestellte(r)*	s.b. who works in an office or a bank	= clerk
working condition	*Arbeitsbedingung*	The trade unions fight for better working conditions.	
workshop	*Werkstatt*	We have to send the broken machine to the workshop.	

3 Working women

vocabulary	dt. Bedeutung	English sentence	syn/opp
(to) be at a disadvantage	*benachteiligt sein*	In most traditional societies, women are at a disadvantage.	
(to) bear the burden	*die Last tragen*	In the Third World women have to bear the burden of the farm and the household.	

vocabulary	dt. Bedeutung	English sentence	syn/opp
career	*Laufbahn, Beruf*	She started her career as a teacher of English.	= vocation, profession, calling
career break	*Unterbrechung der beruflichen Tätigkeit*	Women who take a career break to look after their children need more financial help.	
career opportunities	*Berufschancen*	job chances	
career women	*Karrierefrau*	a woman who is more interested in her professional career than in being a housewife and mother	
DINKs	*Abk. für kinderlose Ehepaare, bei denen beide verdienen*	**d**ouble **i**ncome **n**o **k**ids	
discrimination	*Benachteiligung*	unfair treatment	= unfairness, prejudice, bias
emancipation	*Befreiung aus sozialer Abhängigkeit; Selbstbestimmung*	For centuries women have fought for their rights and emancipation.	= liberation
(to) enter on a career	*eine Laufbahn einschlagen*	Marian wants to enter on a career as a fashion model.	
equal pay	*gleiche Bezahlung*	In the United States, equal pay has been the law since 1963.	
equality	*Gleichheit*	Toleration and equality are necessary for people in order to live in harmony.	≠ inequality
equality of the sexes	*Gleichbehandlung der Geschlechter*	equal (and fair) treatment of men and women	

vocabulary	dt. Bedeutung	English sentence	syn/opp
(to) get to the top (of one's profession)	*Karriere machen*	Working women find it hard to get to the top.	
(to) give up one's career	*seinen Beruf aufgeben*	Alice gave up her career as a teacher when she had her first baby.	
incompatible	*unvereinbar*	Working long hours is incompatible with family life.	= unsuited ≠ compatible, suited
independent of	*unabhängig von*	Modern women want to be economically and psychologically independent of men.	≠ dependent
inequality	*Ungleichheit*	the unfair difference between groups of people in society	≠ equality
low-paying job	*niedrig (schlecht) bezahlte Arbeit*	Around the world, women are more likely than men to hold low-paying jobs.	
low-wage job	*niedrig (schlecht) bezahlte Arbeit*	In France, 25 % of working women hold low-wage jobs – 8 % of men do.	≠ high-wage job
male dominance	*männliche Vorherrschaft*	The times of male dominance in the labour market are not yet over.	
male-dominated	*von Männern beherrscht*	Many women find it hard to get to the top in a male-dominated business world.	
part-time job	*Teilzeitarbeit*	Young mothers are often eager for part-time jobs that allow them to combine work with child-rearing.	≠ full-time job

vocabulary	dt. Bedeutung	English sentence	syn/opp
part-timer	*Teilzeitkraft*	The number of women in work has increased in recent years; many are part-timers.	
pay scale	*Tarif, Lohnskala*	Women hold jobs at the bottom of the pay scale.	
quota	*Anteil*	The quota of women on company boards is still rather low.	= share, percentage
(to) recruit	*einstellen, anwerben*	Although male and female university graduates are recruited in equal numbers, fewer women make it to the top.	
self-assertion	*Selbstbehauptung, Durchsetzungsvermögen*	Single mothers developed greater independence and self-assertion.	
self-assured	*selbstsicher*	More and more self-assured women manage top jobs.	= confident, assured
self-realization	*Selbstverwirklichung*	Women choose a profession in the hope of personal and economic self-realization.	
subordination	*Unterordnung*	In the Middle Ages, feudal law (*Feudalrecht*) encouraged the subordination of women to men.	
two-earner household	*Haushalt, in dem zwei verdienen*	Britain has more two-earner households than before, but still too many no-earner households.	
workforce	*Belegschaft*	In 1990, women were at least one-third of the workforce in most countries.	= staff, personnel, human resources

4 Trade unions

vocabulary	dt. Bedeutung	English sentence	syn/opp
(to be) anxious	*auf etw. bedacht sein*	The employers are anxious to reach a compromise with the workers who are on strike.	= keen, eager
blackleg	*Streikbrecher*	A blackleg usually has to suffer a lot of insults from workers who are out on strike.	= strike breaker
(to) call a strike	*einen Streik ausrufen*	The General Workers' Union will probably call a strike.	
collective bargaining [Pl.]	*Tarifverhandlungen*	The employers and the unions have entered into collective bargaining.	
consensus	*Übereinstimmung*	the opinion of all or most of the people consulted	= agreement, consent
industrial action	*Streik*	The union members voted against industrial action.	
(to) lock out	*aussperren*	The managers decide today whether they will lock out the workers who are on strike.	
negotiation	*Verhandlung*	If negotiations fail the printers will go on strike and there won't be any newspapers tomorrow.	= talks
picket	*Streikposten, Streikwache*	The printers' union placed pickets at the factory gates to make sure that no worker would break the strike.	
shop steward	*gewerkschaftlicher Vertrauensmann*	In our printing plant, Joe Cooper is the shop steward of the printers' union.	

vocabulary	dt. Bedeutung	English sentence	syn/opp
strike	*Streik*	If the employers don't pay us more, there will be a strike soon.	= walkout
strike vote	*Urabstimmung*	The union must carry out a strike vote among its members before it can call a strike.	
trade union	*Gewerkschaft*	In the 19th century the first trade union was formed.	= labor union [US]
wildcat strike	*wilder (illegaler) Streik*	If the union doesn't carry out a vote before a strike, the strike is illegal: it's a wildcat strike.	

5 Managing finances

vocabulary	dt. Bedeutung	English sentence	syn/opp
account	*Konto*	I'd like to open an account, please.	
account holder	*Kontoinhaber*	The bank was accused of selling personal details of account holders to other firms.	
application form	*Antragsformular*	I will complete the application form for you.	
ATM (automated teller machine) [US]	*Geldautomat*	At most banks there is an ATM in the lobby.	
bank charges	*Bankspesen*	Bank charges have gone up a lot lately.	
bank clerk	*Bankangestellter*	I'm working as a bank clerk with the NatWest in Bromley.	

vocabulary	dt. Bedeutung	English sentence	syn/opp
bank manager	*Bankdirektor*	Could I speak to the bank manager, please?	
bankrupt	*bankrott, zahlungsunfähig*	Many tradesmen go bankrupt because the building contractors don't pay their bills.	
bankruptcy	*Bankrott*	Due to the rise in the oil price many companies were facing bankruptcy.	
beneficiary	*Begünstigte(r), Nutznießer*	The beneficiary is the person who receives the money from a trust or an insurance policy.	
BIC (bank identifier code)	*Bankleitzahl*	For money transfers you must know the recipient's IBAN and BIC.	
bill	*[AE] Banknote*	I haven't got any $ 20 bills on me.	
	[BE] Rechnung	Can I have the bill, please?	
branch	*Filiale, Zweigstelle*	a local office of a large business or bank	
break-even point	*Gewinnschwelle, Kostendeckungspunkt*	Airliners have a break-even point, at a load of about 70 % of capacity.	
(to) cancel	*kündigen, auflösen*	A standing order runs until you cancel it.	= to annul
cash dispenser/ cash point [UK]	*Geldautomat*	You can operate the cash dispenser with your Eurocard.	= cash machine, ATM
cashier ([US] teller)	*Kassierer(in)*	a person handling money in a bank or shop	
charge	*Gebühr*	The bank offers: no charge on overdrafts of up to £ 100.	= fee

vocabulary	dt. Bedeutung	English sentence	syn/opp
checking account [US]	*Girokonto ohne Dispositionskredit*	In the USA normal current accounts are known as checking accounts.	= current account [UK]
cash on delivery (COD)	*per Nachnahme*	The merchandise you ordered must be paid cash on delivery.	
(to) credit	*gutschreiben*	On a German statement an "H" next to the amount means that the sum was credited to you.	
credit balance	*Guthaben*	The bank pays 0.5 % on credit balances of 10,000 euros and over.	
credit limit	*Dispositionskredit, Kreditlinie*	The bank informs you of your credit limit.	
creditor	*Gläubiger*	a person or company to whom you owe money	≠ debtor
current account	*Girokonto, Kontokorrentkonto*	I keep my current account with Barclays Bank.	
(to) debit	*belasten, abbuchen*	On a German statement an "S" next to the amount means that the sum was debited from you.	
debit balance	*Sollsaldo*	Interest must be paid on any debit balance that your account shows.	
debit entry	*Sollbuchung*	On a German statement a debit entry is marked with an "S".	
debtor	*Schuldner*	s.o. who owes money	
direct debit authorization	*Einzugsermächtigung*	With a direct debit authorization you authorize s.o. to debit your account.	

vocabulary	dt. Bedeutung	English sentence	syn/opp
direct debiting	*Einzugs-, Abbuchungs-, Lastschriftverfahren*	Can you explain how direct debiting works?	
(to) disclose	*bekannt geben, verraten*	You mustn't disclose your PIN to anyone!	= to reveal ≠ to conceal, to hide
exchange rate	*Wechselkurs*	The exchange rate tells you how much you have to pay to buy a foreign currency.	
foreign exchange	*Devisen*	Meryl has been employed in the foreign exchange department of the Hong Kong and Shanghai Banking Corporation since 2001.	
(to) grant (a credit)	*(einen Kredit) gewähren*	Banks grant credits to their customers.	= to give
IBAN (international bank account number)	*internationale Bankkontonummer*	For money transfers you must know the recipient's IBAN and BIC.	
(to) insert	*(Karte bei Automaten) einführen*	Please insert your card into the slot.	
interest [Sg.]	*Zins(en)*	Investors want their money to earn interest.	
investor	*(Geld-)Anleger*	Banks deal in securities for investors.	
joint account	*gemeinsames Konto*	My wife and I have a joint account.	
letter of credit	*Kreditbrief, Akkreditiv*	authorization made by a buyer to his agent (usually a bank) to make payment to a seller	
loan	*Darlehen, Kredit*	money (borrowed from a bank) for which you have to pay interest	= credit

vocabulary	dt. Bedeutung	English sentence	syn/opp
marital status	*Familienstand*	What's your marital status, please?	
means of payment	*Zahlungsmittel*	The most popular means of payment in the USA is by credit card.	
mortgage	*Hypothek, Verpfändung*	The Johnsons found it hard to repay their mortgage.	
non-cash	*bargeldlos*	Most firms prefer non-cash payment.	
online banking	*Internet-, Online-banking*	Banks inform customers of the advantages of online banking.	= electronic/ Internet banking
overdraft	*Kontoüberziehung, Kontokorrentkredit, Dispositionskredit*	Banks lend money to their customers by granting overdrafts.	
(to) overdraw	*sein Konto überziehen*	Be careful not to overdraw your account too much.	
overheads	*laufende Geschäftskosten, Gemeinkosten*	business expenses (such as rent, insurance, or heating)	
PIN (personal identification number)	*persönliche Geheimzahl*	a number given to a bank customer so that he can use the cash machine	
plc (public limited company)	*AG (Aktiengesellschaft)*	This offer comes to you from The Royal Bank of Scotland plc.	
power of attorney	*Vollmacht*	the authority to act in your name	
(to) raise (capital, money)	*(Kapital) aufbringen*	Banks help companies to raise capital for financing.	
reminder	*Mahnung*	If customers don't pay their debts, firms have to send off one or two reminders.	

vocabulary	dt. Bedeutung	English sentence	syn/opp
(to) retain	*zurückbehalten, einziehen*	Cash dispensers retain cards if an incorrect PIN has been punched three consecutive times.	
revenue	*Einnahmen, Erlös*	money received or gained	= income
savings account	*Sparkonto*	You can earn more interest if you keep your money in a savings account.	
securities [Pl.]	*Wertpapiere, Effekten*	Banks deal in securities for investors.	
specimen signature	*Unterschrifts-probe*	Please give us a specimen signature on this form.	
standing order	*Dauerauftrag*	Most people pay their rent by standing order.	
statement	*(Konto-)Auszug*	The bank advises its customers to check their bank statements carefully.	
TAN (transaction authentication number)	*TAN (Transaktions-nummer)*	To be on the safe side use a mobile TAN when you do online banking.	
(to) transfer	*überweisen*	Firms such as PayPal transfer money securely through the Internet.	
VAT (value added tax)	*Mehrwertsteuer*	Our prices include VAT and postage.	
(to) withdraw	*(Geld) abheben*	to take out money of an account	
withdrawal	*Abhebung*	You should inform your bank in advance if you wish to make a large cash withdrawal.	

Agriculture and developing countries

1 Agriculture

vocabulary	dt. Bedeutung	English sentence	syn/opp
abundant	*reichlich*	The fertile areas of the US have abundant rainfall.	= plentiful
agriculture	*Landwirtschaft*	In the USA, agriculture has always played a major role in the economy.	= farming
alternative farming	*biologische Landwirtschaft*	Alternative farming has grown in importance.	= chemical-free farming
(to) apply to	*an-, verwenden*	Farmers should apply fewer pesticides to their crops.	
arable farming	*Ackerbau*	The soil in the Great Lakes area is less suited to arable farming.	
chemical-free farming	*biologische Landwirtschaft*	Chemical-free farming methods can be just as productive as traditional ones.	= alternative farming, non-chemical farming
climate	*Klima*	general weather conditions typical of a place	
corn [AE]	*Mais*	The Corn Belt stretches from the Allegheny Mountains to Missouri.	= maize [BE]
crop	*Feldfrucht, Saat, Gesamternte*	plants that are grown in large quantities for food	
dairy belt	*Milchwirtschaftsgürtel (USA)*	The Dairy Belt extends through New England and the Great Lakes area.	

vocabulary	dt. Bedeutung	English sentence	syn/opp
dairy farming	*Milchwirtschaft*	Thousands of farmers depend on the price of milk for their dairy farming produce.	
dairy produce	*Milch-, Molkereiprodukte*	foods that are made from milk	
(to) devastate	*vernichten, verwüsten*	Heavy storms and floods devastated much of the country's fertile land.	= to ruin, to destroy
(to) exhaust	*erschöpfen, auslaugen*	Inefficient farming methods have exhausted the soil.	
fertile **fertility**	*fruchtbar* *Fruchtbarkeit*	producing or bearing fruit in great quantities	≠ infertile, barren
fertilizer	*Dünger*	Fertilizers are used to revitalize the soil.	
food safety	*Sicherheit der Nahrung*	Public concern about the safety of our food has increased since the arrival of genetically modified foods.	
GM (genetically modified)	*gentechnisch verändert*	GM soya is commonplace in the USA.	
grain	*Korn(art), Getreide(art)*	The rotation of corn with other grain keeps the soil fertile.	= cereal
granary	*Kornkammer*	a region producing large quantities of corn	
growing season	*Wachstums-, Reifezeit*	In the Great Lakes area the growing season is rather short.	
harvest	*Ernte(zeit)*	time of year when the agricultural crops are gathered	
herbicide	*Unkrautbekämpfungsmittel*	a chemical needed to destroy weeds	

vocabulary	dt. Bedeutung	English sentence	syn/opp
level land	*Flachland*	The Corn Belt occupies the USA's largest continuous area of fertile level land.	
livestock	*Vieh*	animals kept or raised on farms	
mixed farming	*Mischlandwirtschaft*	The Corn Belt has a genuine mixed farming system.	
moist	*feucht*	slightly or moderately wet	= damp, humid
nutrient	*Nährstoff*	Rotation of crops keeps nutrients in the soil naturally.	
pasture	*Weide, Weidefläche*	land covered with grass	
pest	*Schädling*	an insect or other animal that attacks crops, food and livestock	
pesticide	*Schädlingsbekämpfungsmittel*	a substance used to destroy insects which harm plants	
primarily	*vorwiegend, hauptsächlich*	The Southern states remained primarily agricultural until after the Civil War.	= mainly, chiefly, above all, predominantly
primary product	*Rohstoff*	Peru sells primary products like minerals and cotton.	= raw material
produce	*landwirtschaftl. Erzeugnisse, Naturerzeugnisse*	The farmer takes his produce to the market every Saturday.	
rotation	*Fruchtwechsel, Abwechslung*	The rotation of corn with other grains preserves the fertility of the soil.	
soil	*Boden*	In the Great Lakes area the soil is less suited to arable farming.	= ground, earth

vocabulary	dt. Bedeutung	English sentence	syn/opp
subsidy	*Subvention*	a sum of money to support farmers and encourage them to grow certain crops	
surplus	*Überschuss*	Farmers should be discouraged from producing surpluses which they cannot market.	
weed	*Unkraut*	a wild plant which grows in a place where it is not wanted	
wheat	*Weizen*	The Wheat Belt is one of the world's chief granaries.	
yield	*Ertrag*	Farmers use fertilizers to increase yields.	

2 Developing countries

vocabulary	dt. Bedeutung	English sentence	syn/opp
appalling	*entsetzlich, erschreckend*	People in the slums live in the most appalling conditions.	= shocking, dreadful, awful
(to) assess	*beurteilen, einschätzen, bewerten*	The commonest way to assess a country's degree of development is by reference to its Gross National Product (GNP).	= to evaluate, to gauge
balance	*Gleichgewicht*	Development policies must aim at a satisfactory balance between population and resources.	= equilibrium
calorie intake	*Kalorieneinnahme, -zufuhr*	The disparity in calorie intake between developing and industrialized countries is not great.	

vocabulary	dt. Bedeutung	English sentence	syn/opp
deficiency	*Mangel*	Vitamin A deficiency can cause night blindness.	= lack, shortage, inadequacy
desert	*Wüste*	Many of these countries are sun-baked deserts where crops do not grow.	
desperate	*verzweifelt*	The majority of people in developing countries live in desperate poverty.	
(to) deteriorate	*sich verschlechtern*	to become worse in condition	
(to be) devoted to	*ausgerichtet auf, gewidmet*	Much of the productive effort of developing countries is devoted to growing food.	= dedicated to
diet	*Kost, Nahrung*	food that a person eats regularly	
disparity	*Ungleichheit, Verschiedenheit*	unfair difference	= imbalance
drought	*Dürre*	a long period during which no rain falls	
family planning	*Familienplanung*	Family planning should be made freely available.	= birth control
fierce	*heftig, scharf, grimmig*	Today a fierce struggle for survival is taking place in developing countries.	= intense, violent
illiteracy	*Analphabetentum*	not knowing how to read or write	
indicator	*Anzeiger, Indikator*	The GNP is still the best single economic indicator of differences between countries.	= gauge [ei]

vocabulary	dt. Bedeutung	English sentence	syn/opp
industrialized nation	*Industrieland*	Setting up factories and providing workplaces has become a necessity for the industrialized nations.	
life expectancy	*Lebenserwartung*	the length of time that people are normally likely to live	
malnutrition	*Unterernährung, schlechte Ernährung*	We have to fight hunger, disease, and malnutrition in developing countries.	
medical care	*medizinische Betreuung, Fürsorge*	Medical care for people living in underdeveloped regions has been improved.	= medical attention
migrant	*Zuwanderer*	a person who moves from one place to another, esp. to find work	
notion	*Vorstellung*	Internet access is an irrelevant notion in societies where even electricity is a luxury.	= idea, view, concept
nutritious	*nahrhaft*	Food intake in the form of meat, dairy produce, fruit and vegetables provides a nutritious diet.	= nourishing
pace	*Schritt, Tempo*	In developing countries, agriculture cannot keep pace with an exploding population.	= rate, speed
peasants [Pl.]	*Kleinbauern*	mostly poor people working on a small piece of land	
population growth	*Bevölkerungswachstum*	Population growth can be controlled by family planning.	

vocabulary	dt. Bedeutung	English sentence	syn/opp
predominantly	*überwiegend*	In poor countries diets are predominantly starchy.	= largely, mainly
prevailing	*(vor)herrschend, bestehend*	It is our duty to abolish the prevailing misery among the poorest people in the world.	= current, existing
(to) rank	*ordnen, einreihen, klassifizieren*	We often rank countries according to their GNP per head of population.	= to rate
rate of mortality	*Sterberate*	The rate of mortality among children in developing countries is very high.	= death rate
(to) rely on	*sich verlassen auf*	People in Africa rely on our contribution to improve their situation.	= to trust, to count on
resources	*Reichtümer eines Landes; Bodenschätze [Pl.]*	manpower and raw materials that a country possesses and can use	= assets
rural	*ländlich*	Most of the undernourished populations of developing countries live in rural areas rather than in towns.	≠ urban
scarce	*knapp, spärlich*	Food-supplies are scarce and more and more people are likely to die of hunger each year.	= rare
sewage	*Abwasser*	There is no sewage system in the slums; that's why often cholera and typhoid break out.	= waste water
shanty town	*Barackensiedlung, -stadt*	collection of rough huts in slum areas	
starchy	*stärkehaltig*	Starchy diets do not provide enough protein.	

vocabulary	dt. Bedeutung	English sentence	syn/opp
starvation	*Hunger*	Every day thousands die of starvation.	= famine, hunger
subsistence	*(Lebens-)Unterhalt*	The poor peasants hardly produce enough food for their own subsistence.	
(to) supplement	*ergänzen*	The GNP is still the best single indicator of differences between countries but it should be supplemented by others.	
(to) surmount	*(eine Herausforderung/ein Problem) meistern*	to overcome a difficulty or an obstacle	
underfed	*unterernährt*	We must not become accustomed to our own prosperity and forget about the underfed millions in poor countries.	= undernourished
unmet need	*ungedeckter Bedarf*	International help must be increased to meet the unmet needs for population programmes.	
urgency	*Dringlichkeit*	In developing countries we are confronted with the urgency to fight hunger, disease, and malnutrition.	
vegetables	*Gemüse*	plants such as cabbages, potatoes, onions	
vicious circle	*Teufelskreis*	We must break the vicious circle between poverty and the rapid population growth.	
widespread	*weit verbreitet*	In the poor countries there are widespread deficiencies of proteins and essential vitamins.	= general

Environment

1 The world around us

vocabulary	dt. Bedeutung	English sentence	syn/opp
balance	*Gleichgewicht*	Species of plants or animals become extinct when human beings upset the balance of nature.	= equilibrium
birth rate	*Geburtenrate*	the number of births for every hundred or every thousand persons	
delicate	*empfindlich*	The earth's biosphere is in a state of delicate balance.	= fragile
drought	*Dürre*	a long period of dry weather; lack of rain	≠ flood
ecology	*Ökologie*	the study of the relationship of plants and animals to their physical and biological environment	
environment	*Umwelt*	the natural world in which people, animals and plants live	= surroundings
environmental studies	*Umweltforschung*	Environmental studies show us how we can save our planet.	
environmentalist	*Umweltschützer*	Environmentalists warn us of the depletion of the ozone layer.	
environmentally aware	*umweltbewusst*	The number of environmentally aware shoppers is increasing.	
equilibrium	*Gleichgewicht*	Too many factories will destroy the ecological equilibrium of the area.	= balance ≠ imbalance

vocabulary	dt. Bedeutung	English sentence	syn/opp
harmful	*schädlich*	causing or likely to cause damage	= damaging, dangerous, unsafe
hazard	*Gefahr*	Smoking is a health hazard.	
hostile	*feindlich*	Many species survive in a hostile environment.	≠ friendly, pleasant
hygiene	*Hygiene*	Hygiene standards in developing countries are low.	
inedible	*ungenießbar*	not suitable for eating	= uneatable
infant mortality	*Kindersterblichkeit*	the percentage of babies or young children who die	
(to) irradiate	*ver-, bestrahlen*	Cancer cells are irradiated so that they cannot spread.	
lead [e]	*Blei*	Lead-free petrol keeps our air clean.	
load	*Last; belasten*	We have loaded our air with dangerous chemicals.	= burden
nutrient	*Nährstoff*	any substance that animals need to eat and plants need from the soil	
overpopulation	*Überbevölkerung*	too many people living in one place	
poisonous	*giftig*	Marine life has been badly affected by the poisonous substances that man has been dumping into the oceans.	= toxic
pollutant	*Schadstoff*	a substance which contaminates the atmosphere	
(to) pollute	*verschmutzen*	to make water, air, soil, etc. dirty	= to contaminate ≠ to clean
polluting	*umweltschädlich*	Less polluting cars will be produced.	

vocabulary	dt. Bedeutung	English sentence	syn/opp
pollution	*Verschmutzung*	In the 1950s and 1960s, nobody thought about pollution.	
preservation	*Erhaltung*	when you keep sth. the same or prevent it from being damaged or destroyed	= conservation
(to) protect	*schützen*	to keep s.o. or sth. safe	= to guard, safeguard
(to) purify	*reinigen*	Trees help to purify the air.	= to cleanse, to filter ≠ to contaminate
quality of life	*Lebensqualität*	Volunteers help to improve the quality of life for poor people in developing countries.	
rain forests	*Regenwälder*	It is feared that by the year 2020 most of the rain forests will have disappeared.	
(to) ravage	*verwüsten*	The uncontrolled growth of algae will ravage fishing grounds.	= to devastate, to wreck
refrigerant	*Kühlmittel*	a substance used for cooling	
resources	*Mittel, Schätze, Ressourcen*	coal, oil and wood are natural resources	
(to) restore	*wiederherstellen*	Environmentalists have worked out plans to restore the natural beauty of the area.	
scarcity	*Knappheit, Mangel*	A scientific report named water scarcity as one of the top global risks in the 21st century.	

vocabulary	dt. Bedeutung	English sentence	syn/opp
solar system	*Sonnensystem*	The earth is different from all the other planets in our solar system.	
species	*Gattung*	Scientists can tell which species of animal early humans hunted and ate.	
supply	*Vorrat*	Germs are a major health hazard in our food supply.	= stock, resource
surface	*Oberfläche*	Greenhouse gas concentrations are responsible for rising temperatures on the earth's surface.	
survival	*Überleben*	continuing to live or exist	
uninhabitable	*unbewohnbar*	not suited for living in	
unleaded [e]	*bleifrei*	Unleaded petrol has made car engines cleaner.	
wildlife activist	*Naturschützer*	a person who cares for the protection of plants and animals	

2 Air pollution

vocabulary	dt. Bedeutung	English sentence	syn/opp
acid rain	*saurer Regen*	Acid rain causes damage to our forests, buildings and rivers.	
aerosol can	*Spraydose*	Paint and hairspray are sold in aerosol cans.	
biosphere	*Biosphäre, Lebensraum*	Our biosphere is in a state of delicate balance.	
carbon dioxide (CO_2)	*Kohlendioxid (CO_2)*	Worldwide CO_2 emissions must be reduced significantly.	

vocabulary	dt. Bedeutung	English sentence	syn/opp
carbon monoxide (CO)	*Kohlenmonoxyd (CO)*	a colourless odourless very poisonous gas	
catalyst	*Katalysator*	London buses were fitted with catalysts in order to reduce nitric oxide (*Stickoxid*) emissions.	
climate	*Klima*	the regular pattern of weather conditions in a certain area	
combustion	*Verbrennung*	Fossil fuel combustion is responsible for global warming.	
(to) contaminate contamination	*verseuchen* *Verschmutzung, Verseuchung*	Dry cleaners using too many chemicals contaminate our air.	= to pollute
depletion	*Verringerung, Schwund*	The depletion of the earth's ozone layer is a major concern of environmentally aware people.	
emission (to) emit	*Ausstoß, Emission* *ausstoßen*	The warming of the earth's atmosphere is the result of the emission of different industrial gases.	
exhaust fumes	*Auspuffgase, Abgase*	Cleaner engines are developed to reduce toxic exhaust fumes.	
fallout	*(radioaktiver) Niederschlag*	Radioactive fallout killed thousands in Hiroshima and Nagasaki.	
global warming	*Erwärmung der Erde*	People have become more aware of the danger of global warming.	
greenhouse effect	*Treibhauseffekt*	global warming of the atmosphere	

vocabulary	dt. Bedeutung	English sentence	syn/opp
hydrocarbon	*Kohlenwasserstoff*	Car manufacturers are reducing hydrocarbon emissions from motor vehicles.	
low-emission	*schadstoffarm*	By 2020 only zero or low-emission cars will be allowed into central London. London introduced the world's first "Ultra Low Emission Zone".	= green (vehicle)
ozone layer	*Ozonschicht*	Holes in the ozone layer and air pollution are growing sources of concern.	
radiation	*Strahlung*	Higher levels of ultra-violet radiation cause skin and other cancers.	
respirable dust	*Feinstaub*	People who are exposed to respirable dust suffer from bronchitis and asthma.	= fine dust
skin cancer	*Hautkrebs*	Larger amounts of ultra-violet light may induce skin cancer.	
soil erosion	*Bodenerosion*	The cutting down of the rain forest will increase soil erosion.	
substitute	*Ersatz(stoff)*	Scientists are trying to find a substitute for the dangerous CFCs *(FCKW)*.	= replacement, alternative
sulphur	*Schwefel*	a yellow chemical substance that has a strong and unpleasant smell	
sulphur dioxide	*Schwefeldioxid*	a poisonous gas that causes air pollution	
ultraviolet rays	*UV-Strahlen*	Ultraviolet rays can cause skin cancer.	

3 Water pollution

vocabulary	dt. Bedeutung	English sentence	syn/opp
ailing	*kränkelnd, dahinsiechend*	We must do sth. to help our ailing oceans.	
detergent	*Reinigungsmittel*	Detergents pollute our rivers.	
(to) discharge	*(Abwasser) einleiten, ablassen*	Too much waste water is discharged into our rivers.	
(to) irrigate	*bewässern*	to provide water for an area of land so that crops can be grown	
sewage	*Abwasser*	waste water from households	
sewage plant	*Kläranlage*	a place where waste water is cleaned	
threat	*Bedrohung*	More attention is being paid to another threat to the seas of the world: algae bloom.	= menace, hazard, risk
(to) threaten	*(be)drohen*	The coastal areas were threatened by flooding.	= to menace ≠ to protect
waste water	*Abwasser*	used water from households or factories	

4 Waste

vocabulary	dt. Bedeutung	English sentence	syn/opp
biodegradable	*biologisch abbaubar*	(of substances) which decompose naturally	= recyclable
disposable bottle	*Einwegflasche*	a bottle which is not returned to the shop and thrown away	

vocabulary	dt. Bedeutung	English sentence	syn/opp
disposal	*Beseitigung*	Special containers are needed for the disposal of harmful rubbish.	
dump	*Müllhalde*	An open dump attracts rats and other pests.	
dumping ground	*Müllhalde, -kippe*	Some nations use the oceans as dumping ground for chemical waste.	
garbage	*Abfall, Müll*	things that we throw away	
junk	*Müll, Abfall*	old things of little value	= trash, litter, refuse
litter	*Müll, Abfall*	pieces of paper and other waste	
nuclear waste	*Atommüll*	The problem concerning the permanent safe dis-posal of nuclear waste is still unsolved.	
packaging	*Verpackung*	Unnecessary packaging can be left in the shops.	
(to) recycle	*wiederverwerten*	to use materials like paper, glass, plastic again	
recycling	*Wiederverwer-tung*	Household waste is sorted in special recycling plants.	
return bottle	*Mehrwegflasche*	a bottle which you return to the shop so that it can be used again	
throw-away	*Wegwerf-*	We must overcome our throw-away mentality.	
toxic waste	*Giftmüll*	Where shall we put our toxic waste?	
waste (to) waste	*Abfall* *vergeuden*	Local district councils are responsible for waste collection.	

vocabulary	dt. Bedeutung	English sentence	syn/opp
waste collection	*Müllabfuhr*	City councils spend a lot of money on waste collection.	= refuse/ rubbish collection
waste disposal	*Müllbeseitigung*	We need safer methods of waste disposal.	
waste manage-ment	*Müllbeseitigung*	organizing the disposal of waste	
waste minimiza-tion	*Müllvermeidung, Müllreduzierung*	The best ways to achieve waste minimization are to reduce packaging and educate consumers about how to throw away less.	
waste separa-tion	*Mülltrennung*	The local council offers a leaflet on waste separation.	

5 Energy

vocabulary	dt. Bedeutung	English sentence	syn/opp
biofuel	*Biokraftstoff*	Crops such as sugar cane and palm oil are the basis of biofuel production.	= renewable/ biomass fuel
conservation (to) conserve	*Erhaltung, Bewahrung* *erhalten*	Little attention has been paid to the conservation of energy.	= preservation, protection
energy con-servation	*Energie-einsparung*	Energy conservation is not a priority in the US.	
energy con-sumption	*Energieverbrauch*	The developed countries are to reduce energy consumption further.	
energy efficiency	*Energieeffizienz, Energieausnut-zung*	The government intro-duced measures to im-prove the energy efficiency of buildings.	

vocabulary	dt. Bedeutung	English sentence	syn/opp
energy transition	*Energiewende*	An energy transition from nuclear to alternative sources is connected with high costs.	
fossil fuel	*fossiler Brennstoff (z. B. Öl, Kohle)*	Cleaner car engines have been developed to curb the burning of fossil fuels.	
fracking	*Fracking*	Fracking is a technology to recover gas from under the earth.	
green energy	*umweltfreund-liche Energie*	Water, wind and solar power are sources of green energy.	= alternative energy
natural gas	*Erdgas*	Natural gas is used for heating houses.	
nuclear power plant	*Atomkraftwerk*	In 1986 a Soviet nuclear power plant at Chernobyl exploded.	
power station	*Kraftwerk*	a place where electricity is generated	
renewable	*erneuerbar*	Wind power is a renewable source of energy.	
reprocessing plant	*Wiederaufberei-tungsanlage*	Demonstrators blocked the entry to the repro-cessing plant at Sellafield.	

Science and technology

1 Genetic engineering

vocabulary	dt. Bedeutung	English sentence	syn/opp
(to) abort	*ein Baby/einen Fötus abtreiben*	to end a pregnancy that is not wanted	
abortion	*Abtreibung*		
(to) abort	*etw. abbrechen*	Due to engine failure the space mission was aborted.	= to cancel, to call off
additive	*Zusatz*	Most of our food contains artificial additives to make it look more appetising and conserve it.	
ailing	*krank, kränkelnd*	giving physical or emotional pain or trouble	= unwell, weak ≠ vigorous
(to) alter	*(ver)ändern*	Genetic engineers alter the inherited characteristics of an organism.	= to change, to modify
application	*Anwendung*	Scientific research and its technological application should be subordinated to moral and spiritual values.	
artificial	*künstlich*	Genetically identical animals were produced artificially.	≠ natural
bacteria [Sg. bacterium]	*Bakterien*	large group of unicellular micro-organisms	
beneficial	*nützlich*	Knowledge of nutrition is beneficial to the health of people.	= advantageous, helpful ≠ harmful, detrimental
benefit	*Nutzen*	Opinions are divided over the potential hazards or benefits of genetic engineering.	

vocabulary	dt. Bedeutung	English sentence	syn/opp
biotechnology	*Biotechnologie*	making use of biological processes for industrial and other purposes	
birth defect	*Geburtsfehler*	a physical or biochemical weakness a person is born with	
by chance	*zufällig*	not intended, unintentionally	≠ intentional
characteristic	*Kennzeichen, Merkmal*	The main characteristic of this plant is that it resists disease.	= feature
cholesterol level	*Cholesterin-spiegel*	A high level of cholesterol in the blood may cause arteriosclerosis (*Arterien-verkalkung*).	
cloning	*Schaffung von erbgleichen Wesen, Klonen*	production of genetically identical individuals by transplanting whole cell nuclei	
(to) combat	*bekämpfen*	High beta-carotene oil is used to combat night blindness.	= to fight against
(to) conduct	*ausführen*	Dangerous experiments can only be conducted under strict safety con-ditions.	= to carry out
(to) contract a disease	*eine Krankheit bekommen, erkranken*	to develop or catch an illness	
(to) convert	*verwandeln*	to change from one form or function to another	
cure	*Heilung*	Genetic engineering offers hope of cures for inherited diseases.	= remedy, medication

vocabulary	dt. Bedeutung	English sentence	syn/opp
(to) decipher	*entziffern*	to succeed in understanding sth. such as a code, an old document etc.	= to decode ≠ to encode
deficiency	*Mangel, Makel, Fehler*	New promising strategies have been developed to help people with a genetic deficiency.	= fault, defect, imperfection
deformed	*missgebildet*	Bernard Marx, a character in Huxley's *Brave New World*, is small and therefore regarded as deformed.	= contorted, crippled
desirable	*erstrebenswert, begehrenswert*	wanted or wished for	
destiny	*Schicksal*	s.o.'s predetermined future	= fate
(to) determine	*entscheiden, bestimmen*	RNA and DNA, the proteins in every cell, determine the basic inherited characteristics of life.	
disease	*Krankheit*	Genetic engineering offers hope of cures for inherited diseases.	= illness
DNA (deoxyribonucleic acid)	*Desoxyribonukleinsäure, DNS*	In 1953, James Watson and Francis Crick demonstrated that genetic material is composed of two nucleic acids, DNA and RNA.	
(to) donate donor	*spenden* *Spender*	People should donate more blood and organs for transplantation.	
embryo	*Embryo, ungeborenes menschliches Wesen*	In 1997 scientists duplicated a human embryo, provoking cries that technology had gone too far.	

vocabulary	dt. Bedeutung	English sentence	syn/opp
embryology	*Embryologie, Forschung an der Entwicklung der befruchteten Eizelle und des Embryos*	the scientific study of the formation and development of embryos	
(to) enhance	*verbessern*	Many spices as well as natural and synthetic flavours enhance the taste of foods.	= to improve
(to) eradicate	*ausrotten*	to destroy completely	= to abolish, to exterminate, to extinguish, to root out ≠ to keep, to preserve, to retain
ethical	*ethisch, sittlich, moralisch*	relating to morals, the science of ethics or standards of conduct	
evolution	*Evolution, Entwicklung*	The present state of all forms of life, from bacteria to humans, has been achieved by evolution.	
extinct	*ausgestorben*	Dinosaurs are extinct.	≠ existent, living
extinct	*erloschen*	The Pacific Rim is an area of active and extinct volcanoes.	
fertile	*fruchtbar*	plants: able to bear fruit; humans: able to conceive a child	≠ infertile, barren
fertilisation	*Befruchtung*	the act or process of impregnating	

vocabulary	dt. Bedeutung	English sentence	syn/opp
(to) fertilize	*befruchten*	Scientists have found ways to fertilize human eggs outside the body.	
food additive	*Lebensmittelzusatz(stoff)*	Dozens of food additives ought to be prohibited as health risks.	
gene	*Gen*	a part of a cell that is passed on from a parent to a child and that controls particular characteristics	
gene technology	*Gentechnologie*	We hope that gene technology will help to treat many inherited diseases.	
genetic code	*genetischer Code*	The complete human genetic code has been deciphered.	
genetic engineering	*Gentechnik*	using technology to change the genes in the cells of plants or animals	
genetically modified food (GM food)	*gentechnisch veränderte Nahrungsmittel*	People have genuine concerns about genetically modified (GM) food.	
geneticist	*Genetiker*	a scientist who has specialised in genetic engineering	
genome	*Genom (= Struktur, Funktion und Regulation menschlicher Gene)*	set of chromosomes: the full complement of genetic information that an individual organism inherits from its parents, e. g. colour of eyes or hair	
genuine	*echt*	Due to medical progress curing hereditary diseases has become a genuine possibility.	= real, true

vocabulary	dt. Bedeutung	English sentence	syn/opp
habitat	*Lebensraum*	the natural home or environment of an animal, plant, or other organism	
haemophilia	*Bluterkrankheit*	It may be possible to cure hereditary diseases such as haemophilia, using gene technology.	
hazard	*Gefahr*	Opinions are divided over the potential hazards or benefits of genetic engineering.	= danger
heredity	*Vererbung*	the passing on of genetic factors such as the colour of hair or eyes from one generation to the next	
human	*menschlich*	Scientists in the USA have experimented with dividing a human embryo.	
hybrid	*Kreuzung, Mischform*	an offspring *(Nachkomme)* of two animals or plants of different races or breeds	
identical	*identisch*	Identical twins are exact copies of one another and develop from the same egg.	
immune	*immun*	protected against and resistant to infection	
impact	*Auswirkung, Einfluss*	Medial progress will have a deep impact on our society.	= effect, consequence
(to) implant	*einpflanzen, implantieren*	Doctors help women have babies by mixing sperm and eggs in a test tube and then implanting the embryos in the womb *(Mutterleib)*.	

vocabulary	dt. Bedeutung	English sentence	syn/opp
implication	*Verwicklung, Auswirkung*	The implications of genetic engineering are not clear to us.	
incurable	*unheilbar*	Diseases considered incurable today will be eradicated in the long run.	
infertile	*unfruchtbar*	There are several treatments open to doctors to try and help infertile couples.	
(to) inherit **inheritance**	*erben* *Erbe*	Genetic engineers alter the inherited characteristics of an organism.	
inherited disease	*Erbkrankheit*	Genetic engineering offers hope of cures for inherited diseases.	= hereditary disease
insemination	*Befruchtung*	The method of artificial insemination is used to help childless couples.	
(to) insert	*einsetzen, einfügen*	Genetic material from one species of plant or animal is inserted into another species.	
(to) isolate	*isolieren*	Scientists can isolate sections of DNA which represent single genes.	
IVF (in vitro fertilisation)	*(wörtlich: Befruchtung im Reagenzglas) künstliche Befruchtung*	In 1978 IVF was first successfully applied to human reproduction.	= artificial insemination
laboratory	*Labor*	a room or building for scientific experiments	
longevity	*Langlebigkeit*	long life, living for a long time	

vocabulary	dt. Bedeutung	English sentence	syn/opp
mammal	*Säugetier*	The first success in cloning an adult mammal was achieved by a team of British researchers in 1996.	
(to) manage	*(etw.) fertig bringen, schaffen*	Scientists managed to divide a human embryo in the early stages of fertilisation.	
(to) manipulate	*bearbeiten, (geschickt) handhaben*	Genetic engineering modifies the characteristics of an organism by manipulating its genetic material.	
mapping	*Gruppenzuordnung*	the act or process of making maps or working out the structures	
metabolism	*Stoffwechsel*	all the chemical processes in the body, esp. those that cause food to be used for energy and growth	
(to) modify	*(ver)ändern*	Genes can be modified with chemicals or radiation.	= to change, to alter
mutation	*Veränderung*	the change in genetic material, e. g. caused by radiation	= alteration, modification
natural selection	*natürliche Auswahl*	Natural selection favours or suppresses a particular gene.	
(to) originate	*entstehen, seinen Anfang nehmen*	Life on earth originated more than 3.4 billion years ago.	= to begin, to start
potential	*möglich*	We have yet to discover the potential risks of genetic engineering.	= possible

vocabulary	dt. Bedeutung	English sentence	syn/opp
pregnant pregnancy	*schwanger* *Schwangerschaft*	Women who have trouble becoming pregnant can turn to methods of artificial insemination.	= expectant, expecting
prenatal	*vorgeburtlich*	before birth, during preg-nancy	
preventive medicine/ treatment	*(Gesundheits-) Vorsorge, Vorsor-gemaßnahme*	Preventive treatment can help avoid chronic diseases.	
primates	*Primaten, Herren-tiere, Säugetier-ordnung (Affen, Menschenaffen, Mensch)*	Primates existed before the dinosaurs became extinct.	
progeny	*Nachkommen*	offspring, children	
promising	*(viel)verspre-chend*	New promising strategies have been developed to help people with a genetic deficiency.	= encouraging
property	*Eigenschaft*	A gene can be reproduced with a medically desirable property.	= characteris-tic, feature
protein	*Protein, Eiweiß*	food such as meat, cheese, fish, or eggs that is neces-sary for the body to renew cells and become strong	
(to) provoke	*hervorrufen*	The experiment with a human embryo provoked great alarm.	= to raise, to stir
(to) refine refinement	*verbessern* *Verbesserung, Verfeinerung*	Scientists have succeeded in refining the technique of cloning.	= to improve
reluctant	*widerwillig, widerstrebend*	to be unwilling to do sth.	= unwilling, hesitant

vocabulary	dt. Bedeutung	English sentence	syn/opp
(to) represent	*darstellen, vertreten*	Scientists can isolate sections of DNA which represent single genes.	
(to) reproduce	*wieder erzeugen, neu bilden; fortpflanzen*	Genes can be reproduced in the laboratory.	= to generate, to duplicate
research researcher	*Forschung* *Forscher*	scientific investigation and study	
(to) resemble	*ähneln*	The earliest existing organisms were cells, resembling modern bacteria.	= to look like
resistant	*widerstandsfähig, immun*	Critics of biotechnology say it could lead to resistant weeds and insects.	
scientist	*Wissenschaftler*	Scientists have to find sponsors for their research work.	
species	*Art, Spezies, Gattung*	Darwin's book *On the Origin of Species by Means of Natural Selection* was published in 1859.	
stem cell	*Stammzelle*	Stem cell research may lead to new treatments for diabetes, Alzheimer's, heart disease and cancer.	
strict	*streng*	Dangerous experiments can only be conducted under strict conditions of containment *(Abschottung)*.	= rigid
supply	*Vorrat, Bestand*	The supply of embryos in fertility clinics is limited.	
test-tube baby	*Retortenbaby*	Louise Brown, born 25 July, 1978, was the first test-tube baby.	

vocabulary	dt. Bedeutung	English sentence	syn/opp
(to) tinker	*herumpfuschen*	Will people wish to eat foods they know have been tinkered with by scientists?	= to mess around, to play around
tissue	*Gewebe*	the material that animals and plants are made of	
topic	*Thema*	Human clones are no longer a topic for science fiction.	= subject, subject matter
(to) transfer	*übertragen*	to move s.o. or sth. from one place to another	
(to) transform	*verwandeln*	Man alone has the power to transform the world he lives in.	= to change, to alter
transplant **(to) transplant**	*Verpflanzung, Transplantation* *verpflanzen*	The South African surgeon Christiaan Barnard performed the first human heart transplant in 1967.	
treatment	*Behandlung*	After treatment in the fertility clinic Mrs Denton had triplets.	
(to) trigger	*etw. auslösen*	An allergy can be triggered by stress or overwork.	= to cause, to bring about, to set off
triplet	*Drilling*	one of three children born at one birth	
variety	*Sorte*	A biotech firm in California has developed a tomato that does not rot as fast as normal varieties.	= sort, kind
vertebrate	*Wirbeltier*	a group of animals (including mammals, birds and fish) with a backbone	

vocabulary	dt. Bedeutung	English sentence	syn/opp
virus	*Virus*	Government research centers in both Canada and the US have decoded the DNA in the suspected SARS (severe acute respiratory syndrome) virus.	

2 Computers

vocabulary	dt. Bedeutung	English sentence	syn/opp
access	*Zugang*	More and more people have access to the Internet.	
account	*Benutzerkonto*	Even the Pope has an account on Facebook.	
app (short for: application)	*Anwendung, Programm, App*	Computer specialists earn good money developing apps for mobile devices.	
cloud	*Cloud (wörtlich: Wolke)*	an image used for the Internet; many users store their data in the cloud.	
compatible	*vereinbar, verträglich, kompatibel*	When you buy a new programme, make sure it is compatible with your computer's operating system *(Betriebssystem)*.	
(to be) computer literate	*Computerkenntnisse besitzen*	to be able to use computers well	
cyber	*Cyber-*	a prefix that is used to relate sth. to the Internet, e. g. -war, -crime, -law	
cybercrime	*Internetkriminalität*	Cyberstalking is an example of cybercrime.	= computer crime

vocabulary	dt. Bedeutung	English sentence	syn/opp
database	*Datenspeicher, Datenbestand*	Every programme on your computer keeps its own database.	
data processing	*Datenverar-beitung*	Data processing is carried out by computers.	
device	*Gerät*	The number of electronic devices people use today has increased enormously.	
feature	*Funktion*	Word processors offer more features than most users need every day.	
file	*Datei*	Think about how to organize your files properly on your hard disk.	
(USB) flash drive	*Speicherstick*	a small stick for storing digital data; it can be connected to a computer through a serial port.	= USB stick
folder	*Ordner*	Save your computer files in different folders on your disk, just like in a box.	
follower	*Anhänger*	Many film stars have millions of followers on Twitter.	
harassment	*Belästigung*	Harassment over the Internet is a serious problem.	
(to) key in	*Daten in einen Computer eingeben*	to enter data with a computer keyboard	
malware (short for: malicious software)	*Schadprogramm*	a software with harmful effects, such as changing or deleting files	
memory	*Speicher*	the capacity of a computer for storing data	

vocabulary	dt. Bedeutung	English sentence	syn/opp
outdated	*veraltet*	Whatever we learn is outdated before we can apply it.	= antiquated, obsolete ≠ up-to-date
(to) paste	*einfügen*	to copy or move text into a document from another text passage or document	
(to) process	*verarbeiten, bearbeiten*	to operate on data by means of a computer programme	
release	*Ausgabe*	Make sure to use the latest release of your anti-virus scanner.	
(to) retrieve	*Informationen abrufen*	to find or extract information stored in a computer	
(to) scan	*durchsuchen*	Use an anti-virus programme to scan your hard disk for malware.	
spreadsheet	*Tabellenkalkulation*	Microsoft's "Excel" is a widely used spreadsheet.	
(to) store	*speichern*	You can store data in the cloud.	
(to) stream	*(kabellos) übertragen*	Netflix streams films over the Internet.	
(to) swipe	*wischen*	On a tablet you swipe with one finger to change pages.	
virus	*Virus*	a software which can reproduce itself and cause great harm to files or other programmes	
wireless	*drahtlos*	Most hotels offer wireless Internet connection.	
word processor	*Textverarbeitung (-sprogramm)*	Microsoft's "Word" is an extremely powerful word processor.	

Media and advertising

1 Television and radio

vocabulary	dt. Bedeutung	English sentence	syn/opp
(to) broadcast	*senden*	Episode 245 of our series will be broadcast next Monday at 9.30 p.m.	= to transmit
cable TV	*Kabelfernsehen*	In cable TV signals are sent along wires, rather than by radio waves.	
CCTV (closed-circuit television)	*Videoüberwachung(ssystem)*	used by police to control inner cities, banks, motorways and other places like football stadiums	
channel	*(Fernseh-)Kanal, Programm*	If you don't like this programme switch over to another channel.	
coverage	*Berichterstattung*	CNN is well-known for its live coverage of world events.	
dish, satellite dish	*Satellitenschüssel*	an aerial (*Antenne*) in the shape of a bowl	
documentary	*Dokumentarfilm*	a film that gives information on a particular subject	
feature	*Spielfilm*	a full-length film, the main film	
feature	*Reportage*	After the news we'll bring you a special feature on drug abuse among young school leavers.	
feedback	*Rückmeldung*	The more feedback we get from viewers, the better.	

vocabulary	dt. Bedeutung	English sentence	syn/opp
live	*direkt*	The final will be shown live on TV.	
network	*Netz, Netzwerk*	The bank uses a computer network to transfer data to all its branches in the country.	
piracy	*das Raubkopieren*	Piracy is a big concern of the digital publishing industry, because digital media can be copied easily.	
ratings	*(Einschalt-)Quoten, Zuschauerzahlen*	Ratings decide whether the series will be continued or not.	
remote control	*Fernbedienung*	With a remote control you can turn on your TV set from where you are sitting.	
satellite	*Satellit*	The new television satellite sends a very strong signal to earth.	
satellite TV	*Satellitenfernsehen*	TV signals are transmitted via satellite.	
screen	*Bildschirm*	Many people maintain that there is too much sex and violence on the screen.	
screenplay	*Drehbuch*	the script of a film	
soap opera	*Seifenoper*	'Coronation Street' is the longest running British TV soap opera.	
sponsor	*Sponsor, Förderer*	a person or an organization that provides the money for a programme or an activity	
subtitle	*Untertitel*	I saw a Spanish film with English subtitles.	

vocabulary	dt. Bedeutung	English sentence	syn/opp
surveillance	*Überwachung*	a close watch kept over s.o. or sth. by a detective or cameras	
(to) tune in	*(ein Programm) einstellen, zuhören*	And don't forget to tune in at 8 o'clock tomorrow when we'll present the 'WORLD 100' best-selling singles of all time.	
(to) turn down	*(Lautstärke) leiser stellen*	Please turn down that terrible noise!	
(to) turn off	*(Radio, TV) ausschalten*	I tried to watch a 'Friends' episode, but after 10 minutes I just had to turn off the set; the acting was pathetic!	= to switch off ≠ to switch on
(to) turn on	*(Radio, Fernseher) an-, einschalten*	With a remote control you can turn on your TV set from where you are sitting.	= to switch on ≠ to switch off
viewer	*(Fernseh-) Zuschauer*	I'm sure the TV viewer doesn't want more and more commercials to interrupt the programmes.	
volume	*Lautstärke*	The volume can be controlled by pressing this button.	
(to) watch TV	*fernsehen*	How many hours a day do you watch TV?	

2 Newspapers and books

vocabulary	dt. Bedeutung	English sentence	syn/opp
advice column	*Ratgeberrubrik, -spalte (in Zeitschriften)*	All women's magazines have at least one advice column.	
appendix	*Anhang (eines Buches); auch: Blinddarm*	A list of hotels is given in the appendix of our tourist guide book.	
brochure	*Broschüre*	a small book or magazine containing pictures and information	= leaflet, pamphlet
censorship	*Zensur*	Especially in times of war there is a strict military censorship on newspaper and TV reports.	
circulation	*(Zeitungs-) Auflage*	The Sun has a daily circulation of about 2 million copies.	
column	*(Zeitungs-) Spalte*	a vertical arrangement of a page or text	
copy	*(Zeitungs-) Exemplar*	I kept a copy of our daily paper with the reports on the German reunification.	
copyright	*Urheberrecht*	Who holds the copyright of the song?	
cover	*(Buch-)Einband*	On the front cover was a picture of a woman in red.	
daily	*Tageszeitung (Kurzform)*	Many Britons read more than one daily.	≠ weekly, monthly
e-book	*E-Book*	book available in electronic form	
edition	*(Buch-)Ausgabe*	This is a valuable first edition of Robert Burns' poems.	

vocabulary	dt. Bedeutung	English sentence	syn/opp
editor	*Redakteur*	a journalist who is responsible for the final version of a text	
electronic publishing	*elektronisches Publizieren*	written information published not on paper but on discs, CD-ROMS or online	= digital publishing
encyclopaedia	*(sehr umfangreiches) Lexikon*	Wikipedia is a free online encyclopaedia.	
e-reader	*Lesegerät für E-Books*	Several multinational corporations compete on the market for e-readers.	
extract	*Auszug*	I hope you'll remember the extract from the US Declaration of Independence which you learnt.	= excerpt
freedom of expression	*Meinungsfreiheit*	Freedom of expression has always been a characteristic of a free and liberal society.	
freedom of the press	*Pressefreiheit*	All democratic states guarantee the freedom of the press.	
front page	*Titelseite*	the first page of a newspaper	
heading	*Überschrift*	Try to find a new heading for this paragraph.	= headline
headline	*Schlagzeile*	the title of a newspaper story	
index	*Register*	an alphabetical list printed at the back of a book	
interference	*(Empfangs-) Störung*	When you listen to the 'Deutsche Welle' in South America you get a lot of interference from foreign broadcasting stations.	

vocabulary	dt. Bedeutung	English sentence	syn/opp
issue	*(Zeitungs-)Ausgabe, Nummer*	In our next issue we'll publish a full report on the latest computer video games.	
leaflet	*Prospekt, Flugblatt*	The bank produced a little leaflet on 'How to open an account with us'.	
letter to the editor	*Leserbrief*	I've never written a letter to the editor in my life.	
manual	*Handbuch*	Why don't you read the instruction manual before you unpack the stereo set, old boy!?	
mass media	*Massenmedien*	Newspapers and TV which reach a great number of people are often referred to as mass media.	
media	*Medien*	the main means of mass communication: newspapers, radio and television	
message	*Nachricht, Botschaft, Mitteilung*	a communication in writing, in speech, or by signals	
national paper	*überregionale Zeitung*	'The Times' is the most famous British national paper.	≠ regional or local paper
news	*Nachricht(en)*	He heard the bad news on the radio.	
newsagent	*Zeitungsladen, -händler*	a shop which sells papers, magazines, sweets and stationery	= paper shop
newsstand	*Zeitungskiosk*	an outdoor place where newspapers are sold	
novel	*Roman*	Stephan King published his first novel *Carrie* in 1973.	

vocabulary	dt. Bedeutung	English sentence	syn/opp
outline	*Übersicht, Umriss, Gliederung*	I'm going to give you a brief outline of the plot of the book *Gone with the Wind.*	
paperback	*Taschenbuch*	a book with a flexible paper binding	
paragraph	*(Text-)Absatz*	a subdivision of an article or essay	
periodical	*Zeitschrift*	a serious – often academic – magazine, e. g. 'The Economist'	
plot	*Handlung, Fabel (eines Romans)*	the main story	
postage	*Briefporto, Postgebühr*	the money you must pay when you send a letter or parcel by post	
(to) publish	*veröffentlichen, herausgeben*	to prepare and issue a book, or piece of music	
publisher	*Verlag, Verleger*	For years I've been trying to find a publisher for my novel *In Sadness We Unite.*	
quality paper	*seriöse Tageszeitung*	The 'Daily Telegraph' is a highly respected quality paper.	≠ tabloid, redtop
quotation	*Zitat*	Every morning our teacher used to greet us with a quotation from Shakespeare.	
(to) quote	*zitieren*	to repeat the exact words somebody said or wrote	
readership	*Leserschaft*	The 'Sun' and the 'Daily Telegraph' cater for a different readership.	
(to) report **report**	*berichten* *Bericht*	The newspapers report every single step of the Royal Family.	

vocabulary	dt. Bedeutung	English sentence	syn/opp
review	*Rezension, Kritik*	a critical evaluation of a book or play	
source	*(Informations-) Quelle*	I've obtained this confidential information from a very reliable source.	
(to) squeeze	*herauspressen, herausquetschen*	The press people tried to squeeze more information from the speaker of the president.	= to obtain
tabloid	*Boulevardzeitung, Klatschzeitung*	a newspaper with small pages, short news stories and a lot of photographs	
volume	*(Buch-)Band*	a book which is part of a work or series	
yellow press	*Sensationspresse*	another name for the tabloids	

3 Advertising

vocabulary	dt. Bedeutung	English sentence	syn/opp
(to) advertise	*inserieren, werben*	Big companies regularly advertise in the national newspapers.	
advertisement, ad, advert	*Anzeige*	a public notice published in the press, on TV or online	
advertising campaign	*Werbekampagne*	The chairman favours the development of a new advertising campaign.	
advertising revenue	*Werbeeinnahmen*	money earned through advertising	
brand	*Marke, Markenbezeichnung*	a product manufactured by a particular company under a particular name	

vocabulary	dt. Bedeutung	English sentence	syn/opp
commercial TV commercial	*Werbesendung, -spot, Fernsehspot*	I like watching commercials on TV, because some of them are quite funny.	
(to) conceal	*verbergen, verstecken, verheimlichen*	Don't try to conceal the whole truth from me.	= to hide
concealed advertising	*Schleichwerbung*	Many readers suspect concealed advertising in shopping articles.	
(to) deceive	*trügen, täuschen*	Bright and colourful packages sometimes deceive the consumers.	= to cheat, to fool, to mislead, to delude
(to) depreciate	*gering schätzen*	You shouldn't depreciate the information offered in public health warnings!	= to devalue, to think little of; ≠ to appreciate
(to) exhibit (at a trade fair) exhibitor	*ausstellen (auf einer Messe)* *Aussteller(in)*	to show goods to the public	
hard sell	*aggressive Verkaufstaktik*	aggressive advertising (often involves applying psychological pressure)	= high pressure selling ≠ soft sell
freebie	*Zugabe, Werbegeschenk*	sth. given away without asking money for it	
(to) ignite	*an-, entzünden, entfachen*	A clever commercial will always ignite a spark in the consumer's mind.	= to arouse the interest
(to) launch	*in den Markt einführen, präsentieren*	The new Porsche model is to be launched in the US next month.	
loss leader	*Lockvogelangebot*	a product which is sold at a loss in order to draw customers	

vocabulary	dt. Bedeutung	English sentence	syn/opp
mail shot	*Direktwerbung (per Post)*	direct advertising by post	
market leader	*Marktführer*	Microsoft is the market leader in office computer programmes.	
market research	*Marktforschung*	Firms invest a lot of money in market research.	
market survey	*Marktuntersuchung*	"How much would you pay for our product?" is a good question for a market survey.	= market research
(to) mislead	*irreführen, betrügen*	If you want loyal customers, don't ever mislead them.	= to cheat, to trick
online advertising	*Werbung im Internet*	Online advertising has become increasingly popular because of its relatively wide reach.	= digital advertising
package	*Verpackung*	The artist M. F. Ginger designed a new package for McCall's new brand of cornflakes.	
potential	*eventuell, möglich*	The company's aim is to find out what colour potential customers would prefer.	
(to) promote promotion	*fördern, steigern, werben für* *Werbeaktion*	With frequent TV appearances the pop star managed to promote sales of his latest album.	
(to) prosecute	*gerichtlich verfolgen*	The Retail Trade Association will prosecute any false trade descriptions.	

vocabulary	dt. Bedeutung	English sentence	syn/opp
questionnaire	*Fragebogen*	a set of written questions to find out people's opinions about a product	
sales rep(resentative)	*Vertreter(in)*	a person travelling around to inform potential customers about his/her firm's product range	
sample	*Muster*	a small part or quantity of a product to show the customer what the complete article is like	
search engine marketing (SEM)	*Suchmaschinenmarketing*	Internet marketing to increase the visibility of websites on search engine result pages	
slogan	*Werbespruch*	The dairy industry was very successful with the slogan "Drink a pint 'a milk a day!"	
social media	*soziale Medien*	Some of the most well-known social media sites include Twitter and Facebook.	
soft sell	*weiche Verkaufstaktik*	the use of suggestion or gentle persuasion in selling	≠ hard sell
(to) suspect	*argwöhnen, vermuten*	Many readers suspect the glossy photos of models in magazines have been digitally enhanced.	
subtle	*fein, feinsinnig*	Advertising has definitely become more subtle.	≠ blatant, crude
(to) target	*abzielen auf, anvisieren*	Businesses spend large amounts of money targeting children with ads.	

vocabulary	dt. Bedeutung	English sentence	syn/opp
target group	*Zielgruppe*	Young people have always been a preferred target group of advertisers.	
video advertising	*Videowerbung*	Video advertising on YouTube has become a profitable source of income for the site's owner Google.	

4 Consumer

vocabulary	dt. Bedeutung	English sentence	syn/opp
bargain	*(gutes) Geschäft, vorteilhafter Kauf*	In the winter sale Mrs Appleton got a real bargain: she bought a coat which was reduced to £ 56.	
best-before-date	*Haltbarkeits-, Verfallsdatum*	McVitie's chocolate biscuits. Best before 28th November.	
brand	*Marke*	a product manufactured by a particular company under a particular name	
brand loyalty	*Markentreue*	buying from the same manufacturer	
branded goods [Pl.]	*Markenartikel*	goods produced by well-known manufacturers which have the manufacturers' label on them	≠ no-name product
cash cow	*Goldesel, umsatzstarkes Produkt*	a product which has been very profitable for a long time	
commodity	*(Handels-)Ware, Gebrauchsartikel*	A large number of commodities bear a guarantee or trade mark.	= article, product, merchandise

vocabulary	dt. Bedeutung	English sentence	syn/opp
(to) compel	*zwingen, verpflichten*	No manufacturer is compelled to give a guarantee.	= to oblige, to force
competitive	*konkurrenz-, wettbewerbsfähig*	The manager believed that the price for the new computer monitor was very competitive.	
competitor	*Konkurrent, Wettbewerber*	We must try to be better than our foreign competitor.	= rival; ≠ partner
(to) conceive	*sich vorstellen, ausdenken, planen, ersinnen*	It's very hard to conceive a better marketing policy for our new product.	= to contrive, to devise
consumer goods [Pl.]	*Verbrauchsgüter, Konsumgüter*	British Standards for consumer goods are rather high.	
consumer guidance	*Verbraucherberatung*	Readers get plenty of consumer guidance in most newspapers and magazines.	
consumer protection	*Verbraucherschutz*	Parliament has seen to it that the new law guarantees better consumer protection.	
dealer	*Händler(in)*	a person or business that buys and sells goods	= merchant, businessman
discernible	*erkennbar*	High quality products are easily discernible as they bear a quality mark stamped on them.	= recognizable, noticeable
discount	*Rabatt*	a reduction in the usual price	= rebate, reduction
(to) dispatch	*absenden, abfertigen*	We shall dispatch the goods you ordered tomorrow.	= to send off

vocabulary	dt. Bedeutung	English sentence	syn/opp
distribution	*Vertrieb*	Our company is using different distribution channels.	
distributor	*Verteiler (Großhändler)*	An important distributor will always try to sell his own brand of goods.	= dealer, trader
(to) evaluate	*auswerten, bewerten, beurteilen*	The chairman began to evaluate the financial situation of the company.	= to assess, to judge
expenses [Pl.]	*Spesen, Geldausgaben*	The representative's travelling expenses are very high this month.	= expenditure
fee	*Gebühr, (Honorar-)Zahlung*	The 'Stiftung Warentest' does not accept fees from manufacturers.	= payment
inaccurate	*nicht zutreffend, falsch, ungenau*	The description on the label of these jeans is inaccurate.	= false, wrong, inexact
irritation	*Verärgerung, Gereiztheit*	The lack of good service in department stores caused for some irritation.	= anger
loyalty	*Treue*	I am convinced of your loyalty to the company.	= faithfulness, fidelity
manufactured goods [Pl.]	*Fertigwaren*	More money is earned with the sale of manufactured goods than with the sale of primary products.	= finished products ≠ raw materials
market share	*Marktanteil*	percentage of the market for a product or service that a company supplies	
(to) mention	*erwähnen*	We should also mention private quality seals when we talk about consumer guidance.	
merchandise	*Handelsware*	goods to be bought and sold	

vocabulary	dt. Bedeutung	English sentence	syn/opp
niche	*Nische*	a specialized but profitable corner of the market	
non-profit	*gemeinnützig*	The German 'Stiftung Warentest' is a non-profit organisation.	
performance	*Leistung*	All our test customers were happy with the performance of the new steam iron.	
preference	*Vorzug, Bevorzugung*	Preference was given to applicants with overseas experience.	
prosperity	*Wohlstand, Gedeihen*	"We are now entering a period of prosperity for all!"	= wealth, economic well-being, affluence ≠ poverty, misery
purchase	*Kauf, Erwerb*	If you ask for a refund, we need to know the exact date of purchase.	= buy, buying
range	*Sortiment, Kollektion*	The little corner shop sells only a limited range of foodstuffs.	= assortment
refund	*Rückzahlung, Rückerstattung*	Without a receipt we cannot guarantee a refund.	
reply coupon	*Antwortschein, Antwortcoupon*	a voucher (Bon) used for prepaying the postage	
response	*Erwiderung, Reaktion, Antwort*	As an immediate response the firm reduced the price of its product by 20 %.	= reply, answer, return
retail price	*Einzelhandelspreis*	the price of a product in the shops	
sales figures	*Verkaufszahlen*	Sales figures have been up by 25 %.	

vocabulary	dt. Bedeutung	English sentence	syn/opp
seal	*Siegel, Bestätigung*	A manufacturer's private seal informs the consumer about the quality of the product.	= signet
sell-by date	*Haltbarkeitsdatum*	The sell-by date informs the customer about the freshness of the product.	
(to) soar	*in die Höhe schnellen, rapide steigen*	As raw materials became more expensive, consumer prices soared.	= to rise, to rocket
standard	*Maßstab, Norm*	Marks and Spencer's standard for the quality of fresh foods is very high.	= norm
stock	*Vorrat, Warenbestand, Warenlager*	We keep more than 35,000 books in stock.	
subscriber	*Abonnent*	A subscriber of the test magazine 'Which' gets valuable information about the quality of a wide range of products.	
transgression	*Übertretung, Vergehen gegen*	Any transgression of the British Retail Trade Standards will be prosecuted.	= violation, offence against
(to) undercut s.b.	*jdn. im Preis unterbieten*	to offer goods or services at a lower price than a competitor	
variety	*Vielfalt, Mannigfaltigkeit*	Consumers today have a variety of products to choose from.	= diversity
wasteful	*verschwenderisch, kostspielig*	We must do something against the wasteful use of scarce resources.	= extravagant
(to) wrap	*(in Papier) einwickeln*	Shall I wrap this book as a present, madam?	

Grundwortschatz

(to) abandon	*aufgeben, preisgeben, verlassen*
ability	*Fähigkeit*
above	*über*
abroad	*ins, im Ausland*
absence	*Abwesenheit*
abundant	*reich, reichlich*
(to) accept	*annehmen*
accident	*Unfall*
(to) accompany	*begleiten*
(to) accomplish	*vollenden, ausführen, (Zweck) erreichen*
according to	*gemäß, nach, entsprechend*
account	*Konto*
(to) account	*Rechenschaft ablegen*
accustomed to	*gewöhnt (an)*
acquaintance	*Bekanntschaft*
(to) acquire	*erlangen, erreichen*
(to) act	*handeln*
(to) add	*zusammenzählen*
(to) address	*ansprechen*
(to) administer	*verwalten*
(to) admire	*bewundern*
admission	*Eintritt*
(to) admit	*zugeben*
(to) advance	*vorrücken*
advantage	*Vorteil*
adventure	*Abenteuer*
advertisement	*(Zeitungs-)Anzeige*
advertising	*Werbung, Reklame*
advice	*Rat(schlag)*
(to) affect	*sich auswirken auf, (Gesundheit) angreifen*
(to) afford	*sich leisten*
agreement	*Vereinbarung*
ahead	*vorn, in Führung*
(to) aim	*zielen*
alive	*lebendig (noch am Leben)*
(to) allow	*erlauben*
ally	*Verbündeter, Bundesgenosse*
almost	*fast, beinahe*
(to) alter	*ändern, sich ändern, verändern*
although	*obwohl, obgleich*
altogether	*insgesamt*
ambition	*Ehrgeiz, Streben*
amount	*Betrag*
amusement	*Unterhaltung, Entzücken*
anchor	*(Schiffs-)Anker*
ancient	*sehr alt*
anger	*Zorn, Ärger, Wut*

angle	*Winkel, Standpunkt*
angry	*zornig*
(to) announce	*ankündigen, bekannt geben*
(to) annoy	*ärgern, belästigen*
annual	*jährlich, Jahres-*
anxiety	*Angst, Besorgnis*
anxious	*gespannt; besorgt*
apart	*getrennt, für sich*
(to) appeal	*1. gefallen, 2. Berufung einlegen, appellieren*
(to) appear	*erscheinen*
appearance	*Erscheinen, Aufkommen*
application	*Bewerbung*
(to) apply for	*sich bewerben um*
(to) appoint	*ernennen*
(to) approach	*sich nähern*
(to) approve	*billigen*
(to) argue	*1. streiten, Einwendungen machen; 2. (das Für und Wider) erörtern, diskutieren*
(to) arise	*sich bieten*
(to) arrange	*vereinbaren*
arrangement	*Vorkehrung*
(to) arrest	*festnehmen*
(to) arrive	*ankommen*
artificial	*künstlich, Kunst-*
(to) ascend	*steigen, aufsteigen, emporsteigen*
ashamed	*beschämt*
(to) ask for	*bitten*
(to) assemble	*sich versammeln*
(to) assert	*behaupten, geltend machen*
(to) assist	*beistehen, helfen, unterstützen*
(to) assume	*glauben, annehmen*
(to) assure	*(jdm. etw.) versichern*
astonished	*erstaunt*
at least	*wenigstens*
(to) attach	*befestigen*
(to) attain	*(Ziel) erreichen, erlangen*
attempt	*Versuch*
(to) attend	*anwesend sein*
attention	*Aufmerksamkeit*
attitude	*Haltung, Einstellung*
(to) attract	*anziehen*
audience	*Publikum*
available	*erhältlich, verfügbar*
average	*Durchschnitt*
(to) avoid	*vermeiden*
aware	*bewusst*
awe	*Ehrfurcht, Scheu, Furcht*
awful	*schrecklich*
baggage [AE]	*Gepäck*

balance	*Gleichgewicht*
bank	*1. Bank (Institut)* *2. Ufer*
bare	*bloß, nackt*
barely	*kaum*
bargain	*Gelegenheitskauf*
(to) bark	*bellen*
bark	*Borke, Rinde*
barrel	*Fass*
base	*Sockel, Basis*
battle	*Schlacht*
bay	*(Meeres-)Bucht*
beak	*Schnabel*
(to) bear	*tragen*
beef	*Rindfleisch*
(to) behave	*sich benehmen*
behaviour	*Verhalten, Benehmen*
behind	*hinten, dahinter, zurück*
belief	*Glaube, Überzeugung*
(to) believe in	*glauben an*
belongings	*Habseligkeiten [Pl.]*
below	*unten, unter*
belt	*Gürtel*
bench	*Bank, Sitzbank*
bench	*(Park-, Garten-)Bank*
(to) bend down	*sich bücken*
benefit	*Nutzen, Vorteil*
beside	*neben*
besides	*außer*
(to) besiege	*belagern*
(to) betray	*verraten, verleiten*
beyond	*jenseits, darüber hinaus*
bill	*Rechnung*
bite	*Bissen, Happen*
blade	*Klinge, Blatt*
(to) blame	*die Schuld geben*
blank	*leer, unausgefüllt, unbeschrieben*
blanket	*Decke, Wolldecke*
blast	*Explosion*
blaze	*(große) Flamme, Feuer*
(to) bleed	*bluten, zur Ader lassen*
(to) bless	*segnen*
block of flats	*Wohnhaus, Mietshaus*
bloodshed	*Blutvergießen*
(to) blush	*erröten, rot werden*
(to) boast	*angeben, prahlen, sich rühmen*
(to) boil	*kochen, abkochen*
bold	*kühn*
bolt	*Bolzen, Riegel, Schraube*
boot	*1. Kofferraum (Auto)* *2. Stiefel*
border	*Grenze*
(to) borrow	*borgen, ausleihen*

bottom	*Grund, unterster Teil, Boden*
bough [aʊ]	*Ast, Zweig*
boundary	*Grenze*
(to) bow [aʊ]	*beugen, neigen*
bow [əʊ]	*(Pfeil und) Bogen*
bowl	*Schale, Schüssel, Napf*
brain	*Gehirn, Verstand, Intelligenz*
branch	*1. Ast (eines Baumes), 2. Zweigstelle*
brave	*tapfer*
breadth	*Breite, Weite*
breath	*Atem*
(to) breathe	*atmen*
(to) breed	*aufziehen, züchten*
brick	*Ziegel*
brief	*kurz, bündig*
bright	*hell*
(to) bring up	*aufziehen, großziehen*
(to) broadcast	*senden, übertragen (TV)*
brook	*Bach*
brow	*Braue, Augenbraue; Stirn*
(to) brush	*bürsten, putzen*
bucket	*Eimer, Kübel*
burden	*Last*
burial	*Begräbnis*
(to) burn	*brennen, verbrennen*
(to) burst	*brechen*
(to) bury	*begraben*
business	*Geschäft*
button	*Knopf*
by birth	*von Geburt*
by mistake	*aus Versehen*
by trade	*von Beruf*
by virtue of	*kraft [Gen.], aufgrund*
campaign	*Feldzug, Wahlkampf*
capability	*Fähigkeit*
capacity	*Fassungsvermögen, Aufnahmefähigkeit*
capital	*Hauptstadt*
(to) capture	*erobern, einfangen*
care	*Sorgfalt*
career	*Karriere, Laufbahn*
carpenter	*Zimmermann*
carpet	*Teppich*
carriage	*Wagen, (Zug-)Waggon*
carve	*(Fleisch) schneiden, zerlegen*
cash	*Bargeld*
(to) cast	*werfen*
cattle	*Vieh*
cause	*Grund, Anlass*
(to) cease	*aufhören, zu Ende gehen*
centre	*Mitte, Zentrum*
century	*Jahrhundert*

certain	*gewiss*
chain	*Kette*
challenge	*Herausforderung*
(to) change	*ändern*
(to) charge	*1. (Geld) verlangen, 2. angreifen*
charged with	*angeklagt wegen*
charity	*Wohltätigkeit; Güte, Nachsicht*
(to) chat	*schwätzen*
(to) cheat	*betrügen, schummeln*
(to) check	*kontrollieren*
cheek	*Backe, Wange*
(to) cheer	*anfeuern*
chief	*oberster, wichtigster, Haupt-*
childhood	*Kindheit*
chill	*Frost, Kälte*
choice	*(Aus-)Wahl*
(to) choke	*würgen, erwürgen, ersticken*
circumstances	*Umstände, Verhältnisse [Pl.]*
citizen	*(Staats-)Bürger*
(to) claim	*beanspruchen*
clearance sale	*Ausverkauf*
clerk	*Angestellter*
(to) combine	*verbinden*
(to) come to terms	*sich einigen*
comfort	*Trost*
commerce	*Handel*
committee	*Ausschuss*
common sense	*gesunder Menschenverstand*
company	*Gesellschaft*
(to) compare	*vergleichen*
(to) compete	*konkurrieren*
(to) complain	*sich beschweren*
(to) complete	*vervollständigen*
(to) conceive	*begreifen*
(to) confess	*gestehen, beichten*
confidence	*Vertrauen*
(to) confirm	*bestätigen, bekräftigen*
(to) confuse	*verwirren*
(to) connect	*verbinden*
conscience	*Gewissen*
conscientious	*gewissenhaft*
conscious	*bewusst*
(to) consider	*betrachten, erwägen*
(to) consist (of)	*bestehen aus*
(to) consult	*um Rat fragen*
(to) consume	*verbrauchen*
(to) contain	*enthalten*
(to) continue	*fortfahren, weitermachen*
convenient	*bequem, günstig*
conversation	*Gespräch*
(to) convey	*befördern, transportieren, bringen*

(to) convince	*überzeugen*
(to) cough	*husten*
counter	*Ladentisch, Theke, Schalter*
courage	*Mut*
court	*Gericht*
crack	*Riss, Spalte*
(to) create	*(er-)schaffen*
crime	*Verbrechen*
critic	*Kritiker*
criticism	*Kritik*
crossing	*Überfahrt*
cruel	*grausam*
cupboard	*Schrank*
curious	*neugierig*
current	*gegenwärtig, aktuell*
curse	*Fluch*
custom	*Sitte, Brauch*
damage	*Schaden*
damp	*feucht, klamm*
danger	*Gefahr*
(to) dare	*wagen*
(to) dawn	*dämmern, tagen*
deaf	*taub*
(to) deal	*austeilen, handeln*
debt	*Schulden*
(to) decay	*verfallen*
(to) deceive	*täuschen*
(to) decide	*entscheiden*
decision	*Entscheidung*
declaration	*Erklärung*
(to) declare	*(öffentlich) erklären*
decline	*Abnahme, Niedergang, Verfall*
deed	*Tat, Heldentat*
defeat	*Niederlage*
defence	*Verteidigung*
(to) defend	*verteidigen*
defy	*trotzen*
degree	*Grad*
delay	*Verspätung*
deliberate	*wohl überlegt, vorsätzlich*
delicate	*zart, zerbrechlich*
delight	*Vergnügen*
(to) deliver	*1. liefern, 2. (eine Rede) halten*
demand	*Nachfrage*
(to) deny	*abstreiten, bestreiten, leugnen*
(to) depart	*abfahren*
(to) depend (on, upon)	*abhängen (von)*
depth	*Tiefe*
(to) derive	*herleiten*
description	*Beschreibung*
(to) deserve	*eine Belohnung verdienen*
desire	*Wunsch*
(to) despair	*verzweifeln*

desperate	*verzweifelt*
(to) despise	*verachten*
(to) destroy	*zerstören*
determination	*Entschlossenheit*
(to) determine	*bestimmen*
(to) develop	*(sich) entwickeln*
device	*Gerät, Vorrichtung*
(to) devote	*widmen*
dictionary	*Wörterbuch*
(to) differ	*sich unterscheiden*
(to) dig	*graben*
dignity	*Würde*
(to) dim	*matt, trüb*
(to) diminish	*vermindern*
(to) direct	*richten*
disadvantage	*Nachteil*
(to) disappoint	*enttäuschen*
(to) discover	*entdecken*
disease	*Krankheit*
(to) disgust	*empören, entrüsten*
dishes	*Geschirr [Pl.]*
(to) dismiss	*entlassen*
display	*(Schaufenster-) Auslage*
(to) dispose	*1. loswerden, 2. verfügen*
(to) dissolve	*auflösen*
distance	*Entfernung*
(to) distinguish	*unterscheiden*
distinguished	*ausgezeichnet, berühmt*
distress	*Elend, Not*
(to) distribute	*verteilen*
(to) disturb	*stören*
(to) divide	*teilen*
domestic	*inländisch, einheimisch*
(to) double	*verdoppeln*
(to) doubt	*(be)zweifeln*
drain	*Abfluss, (fig.) Abwanderung*
draught	*Luftzug, (Durch-)Zug*
(to) draw	*(Schlussfolgerungen) ziehen*
drop	*Fall, Sturz*
(to) drown	*ertrinken, ertränken*
due to	*infolge*
dull	*1. schwerfällig, langweilig; 2. stumpf (Messer)*
dust	*Staub*
duty	*Pflicht*
eager	*begierig*
(to) earn	*Geld verdienen*
earnest	*ernsthaft, sorgfältig*
ease	*Bequemlichkeit, Ruhe*
economic	*wirtschaftlich*
economical	*sparsam, wirtschaftlich*
edge	*Rand, Kante*

(to) edit	*(Text) herausgeben, redigieren*
education	*Ausbildung*
effect	*Wirkung*
efficiency	*Tüchtigkeit*
effort	*Anstrengung*
election	*Wahl*
electricity	*Elektrizität*
(to) employ	*beschäftigen, anstellen*
(to) enclose	*(einem Brief) beilegen*
(to) encourage	*ermutigen*
enemy	*Feind*
engaged	*1. belegt, besetzt; 2. verlobt*
engine	*Motor*
(to) entertain	*unterhalten*
entire	*ganz*
entrance	*Eingang*
equal	*gleich*
equality	*Gleichheit*
(to) escape	*entfliehen*
essential	*wesentlich, notwendig*
established	*gegründet*
even	*sogar*
event	*Ereignis*
evil	*übel, böse*
exact	*genau*
(to) examine	*untersuchen*
except	*außer*
exception	*Ausnahme*
(to) exchange	*tauschen*
existence	*Dasein, Leben*
expense	*Kosten*
experience	*Erfahrung*
experiment	*Versuch*
(to) explain	*erklären*
explanation	*Erklärung*
(to) explore	*erforschen*
(to) extend	*verlängern*
extension	*Verlängerung*
extent	*Ausmaß, Umfang*
fact	*Tatsache*
factory	*Fabrik*
(to) fade	*verblassen*
(to) fail	*(bei einer Prüfung) durchfallen*
failure	*Misserfolg*
faint	*schwach*
faith	*Glaube*
faithful	*treu*
false	*falsch*
familiar	*vertraut*
fare	*Fahrgeld*
fashion	*Mode*
fast	*schnell*
(to) fasten	*festmachen*
fate	*Schicksal*
fault	*Fehler*

favour	*Gefälligkeit*
favourable	*günstig*
favourite	*Lieblings-*
fear	*Angst*
feather	*Feder*
fence	*Zaun*
fertile	*fruchtbar*
fever	*Fieber*
fierce	*wild, scharf, heftig*
final	*endgültig*
finally	*schließlich*
fine	*Geldstrafe*
firm	*Firma*
fist	*Faust*
(to) fit	*passen*
flake	*Flocke*
flat	*flach*
(to) flatter	*schmeicheln*
flavour	*Geschmack*
(to) flee	*fliehen*
(to) float	*(an der Oberfläche) schwimmen*
flock	*Herde*
(to) flood	*überfluten*
flour	*Mehl*
(to) flourish	*blühen, gedeihen*
(to) fold	*falten*
for good	*endgültig*
(to) forbid	*verbieten*
force	*Gewalt*
forehead	*Stirn*
foreign	*ausländisch*
(to) foretell	*vorhersagen*
fork	*Gabel*
former	*früher, ehemalig*
fortunate	*glücklich*
fortune	*Vermögen*
frame	*Rahmen*
free of charge	*kostenlos*
(to) freeze	*(er)frieren, gefrieren, erstarren*
frequently	*oft*
fright	*Schrecken, Schreck*
frontier	*Grenzland, Grenze*
(to) frown	*die Stirn runzeln*
(to) fry	*braten*
fun	*Spaß*
(to) furnish	*möblieren, ausstatten*
furniture	*Möbel*
fury	*Raserei, Wut*
(to) gain	*gewinnen, profitieren*
game	*Spiel*
gas [AE]	*Benzin*
(to) gasp	*keuchen*
gate	*1. Tor, Sperre; 2. Flugsteig*
(to) gather	*sich versammeln*
gay	*1. homosexuell; 2. lustig, vergnügt*

general	*allgemein*
generally	*im Allgemeinen*
generous	*großzügig*
gentle	*sanft, leicht*
(to) get rid of	*loswerden*
(to) get up	*aufstehen*
(to) get used to	*sich gewöhnen an*
giant	*riesig*
gift	*Gabe, Begabung*
(to) give a hand	*behilflich sein*
(to) give up	*aufgeben, aufhören*
glad	*froh*
glance	*(flüchtiger) Blick*
glasses [Pl.]	*Brille*
glorious	*glorreich, prächtig*
glory	*Ruhm*
glove	*Handschuh*
good-bye	*Auf Wiedersehen, Lebewohl!*
goods	*Waren*
(to) govern	*regieren*
government	*Regierung*
gradually	*allmählich*
grain	*Getreide, (Samen-)Korn*
(to) grant	*gewähren, bewilligen*
grateful	*dankbar*
grave	*Grab*
greeting	*Begrüßung, Gruß*
grief	*Gram, Kummer*
(to) grow	*wachsen*
growth	*Wachstum*
(to) guard	*bewachen*
(to) guess	*(er)raten, vermuten*
guest	*Gast*
guilt	*Schuld; Strafbarkeit*
habit	*Gewohnheit, Angewohnheit*
half	*halb; Hälfte*
hall	*Diele*
ham	*Schinken*
(to) handle	*handhaben, behandeln*
handsome	*gut aussehend, hübsch*
(to) happen	*sich ereignen*
harbour	*Hafen*
hardly	*kaum*
harm	*Schaden*
harvest	*Ernte*
haste	*Eile*
hate	*Hass*
health	*Gesundheit*
heap	*Haufen*
heat	*Hitze*
(to) hide	*verbergen*
(to) hire	*mieten*
history	*Geschichte*
hole	*Loch*
hollow	*hohl*

holy	*heilig*
honest	*ehrlich*
honour	*Ehre*
however	*jedoch*
human	*menschlich*
(to) hunt	*jagen*
(to) hurry	*sich beeilen*
husband	*(Ehe-)Mann*
idea	*Vorstellung*
ideal	*vorbildlich*
idle	*untätig*
(to) imagine	*sich vorstellen*
immediate	*unmittelbar, sofort*
immense	*ungeheuer, unermesslich*
importance	*Wichtigkeit*
impossible	*unmöglich*
impression	*Eindruck*
(to) improve	*verbessern*
improvement	*Verbesserung*
(to) include	*einschließen, enthalten*
(to) increase	*zunehmen*
indeed	*in der Tat, gewiss*
independent	*unabhängig*
inferior	*untergeordnet, minderwertig*
influence	*Einfluss*
(to) inform	*benachrichtigen*
(to) inquire	*sich erkundigen*
inquiry	*1. Anfrage, 2. offizielle Untersuchung*
inside	*drinnen*
(to) insist (on)	*(auf etw.) bestehen*
instead	*stattdessen*
instruction	*Anweisung, Gebrauchsanweisung*
(to) intend	*beabsichtigen*
intention	*Absicht*
interest	*1. Interesse, 2. Zins*
(to) interrupt	*unterbrechen*
(to) introduce	*(jdn., sich) vorstellen*
(to) invent	*erfinden*
invention	*Erfindung*
invitation	*Einladung*
(to) invite	*einladen*
(to) iron	*bügeln*
iron	*Eisen*
irregular	*ungleichmäßig, uneben*
island	*Insel*
issue	*Streitfrage*
jam	*Marmelade*
jealous	*eifersüchtig*
jealousy	*Eifersucht*
jewel	*Edelstein*
job	*Stellung, Arbeitsstelle*
(to) join	*sich anschließen, beitreten*
joint	*Gelenk*

joke	*Witz*
journey	*Reise*
judge	*Richter*
judgement	*1. (Gerichts-)Urteil 2. Beurteilung, Urteil*
juice	*Saft*
justice	*Gerechtigkeit*
(to) justify	*rechtfertigen*
(to) kick	*treten*
kind	*freundlich, liebenswürdig*
kindness	*Freundlichkeit, Liebenswürdigkeit*
kingdom	*Königreich*
knife	*Messer*
knot	*Knoten*
knowledge	*Kenntnisse, Wissen*
labour	*Arbeit*
lack	*Mangel*
ladder	*Leiter*
lake	*(Binnen-)See*
lame	*lahm*
language	*Sprache*
late	*spät*
laughter	*Gelächter*
(to) lay	*legen; (den Tisch) decken*
leaf	*Blatt*
(to) lend	*etw. verleihen*
length	*Länge*
level	*Höhe, Niveau*
library	*Bücherei*
(to) limit	*begrenzen*
liquid	*Flüssigkeit*
load	*Last*
local	*örtlich*
lock	*(Tür-)Schloss*
loose	*locker*
(to) lose	*verlieren*
loss	*Verlust*
low	*niedrig; leise (Stimme)*
lungs [Pl.]	*Lunge*
mail	*Post*
main	*Haupt-*
management	*(Geschäfts-)Führung, Verwaltung*
manager	*Leiter, Direktor*
manners	*Manieren*
marks	*(Schul-)Noten*
marriage	*Heirat, Ehe*
mass	*1. Masse 2. (kirchliche) Messe*
(to) match	*(farblich) passen*
meadow	*Wiese*
meaning	*Sinn, Bedeutung*
means [Pl.]	*Mittel*
measure	*Maß, Maßnahme*
mechanic	*Mechaniker*
(to) melt	*schmelzen*

memory	Gedächtnis
(to) mention	erwähnen
merchant	(Groß-)Kaufmann
mercy	Gnade, Mitleid
mere	bloß
merely	nur, bloß
message	Nachricht, Botschaft
mill	Mühle, Fabrik
mind	Sinn, Verstand
mine	Bergwerk
misery	Elend, Not
(to) miss	verpassen
model	Modell
moderate	mäßig, gemäßigt
modest	bescheiden
movement	Bewegung
mud	Schlamm
murder	Mord
muscle	Muskel
mysterious	geheimnisvoll
mystery	Geheimnis, Rätsel
narrow	eng, schmal
native	einheimisch, (Ur-)Einwohner
necessity	Notwendigkeit
need	Bedürfnis, Bedarf
(to) neglect	vernachlässigen
neighbourhood	Nachbarschaft
neither	keine(r, s)
nephew	Neffe
news [Pl.]	Nachricht
niece	Nichte
noble	edel, großzügig
nor	auch nicht
not yet	noch nicht
(to) note	beachten
nowadays	heutzutage
oak	Eiche
(to) object	Einspruch erheben
objection	Einwand
(to) observe	beobachten
occasion	Anlass
occupation	Beschäftigung
(to) occupy	1. (sich) beschäftigen 2. besetzen
offence	Vergehen
(to) offend	beleidigen
offer	Angebot
opinion	Meinung
opportunity	(günstige) Gelegenheit
opposite	gegenüber
opposition	Widerstand
order	Auftrag
ordinary	gewöhnlich
(to) organize	organisieren
origin	Ursprung
otherwise	sonst

out of work	*arbeitslos*
outline	*Umriss*
(to) overcome	*überwinden*
(to) owe	*schulden*
owner	*Besitzer*
pack	*Rudel*
pain	*Schmerz*
painful	*schmerzhaft*
pale	*bleich*
pardon	*wie bitte?*
particularly	*besonders*
party	*Partei*
(to) pass (by)	*vorbeigehen (an)*
passenger	*Reisender, Fahrgast*
past	*vorüber, vorbei*
patience	*Geduld*
payment	*Zahlung, Bezahlung*
peculiar	*eigentümlich*
pencil	*Bleistift*
perfect	*vollkommen*
performance	*Vorstellung, Aufführung*
permission	*Erlaubnis*
(to) persuade	*überreden*
petrol	*Benzin*
(to) pick	*(Früchte) pflücken*
pigeon	*Taube*
pile	*Haufen, Stoß*
pin	*Stecknadel*
pity	*Mitleid*
plain	*einfach, schlicht*
plant	*1. Pflanze* *2. Fabrikanlage, Werk*
plate	*Teller*
pleasant	*angenehm*
pleasure	*Vergnügen*
poison	*Gift*
(to) polish	*polieren*
polite	*höflich*
political	*politisch*
politics	*Politik*
popular	*beliebt*
population	*Bevölkerung*
port	*Hafen(stadt)*
position	*Stellung, Lage*
(to) possess	*besitzen*
possession	*Besitz*
possibility	*Möglichkeit*
(to) post	*auf die Post geben*
pot	*Kanne*
(to) present	*überreichen, schenken*
(to) press	*bügeln*
pressure	*Druck*
(to) pretend	*vorgeben, so tun als ob*
(to) prevent	*abhalten (von), hindern (an)*
price	*(zu bezahlender) Preis*
pride	*Stolz*

prison	*Gefängnis*
prize	*(Sieges-)Preis*
probable	*wahrscheinlich*
profession	*Berufsstand, höherer Beruf*
profit	*Gewinn*
progress	*Fortschritt*
promise	*Versprechen*
(to) pronounce	*aussprechen*
pronunciation	*Aussprache*
proof	*Beweis*
proper	*passend, richtig, geeignet*
property	*Eigentum, Grund-stück*
proposal	*Vorschlag*
(to) propose	*vorschlagen*
(to) protect	*(be)schützen*
proud	*stolz*
(to) prove	*beweisen*
(to) provide	*sorgen (für), ver-sorgen*
public	*öffentlich*
(to) punish	*bestrafen*
punishment	*Strafe*
purpose	*Absicht, Zweck*
puzzle	*(Kreuzwort-)Rätsel*
quantity	*Menge*
quarrel	*Streit*
quite	*ganz, ziemlich*

race	*Rasse; Rennen*
(to) raise	*1. (Frage) aufwerfen, 2. (Stimme) erheben*
range	*Auswahl*
rank	*Rang*
rare	*selten*
rate	*Quote, Anteil; Ver-hältnis*
rather	*lieber*
raw	*roh*
reason	*Grund, Anlass*
reasonable	*vernünftig, ange-messen*
recent	*jüngst, neu*
(to) recommend	*empfehlen*
(to) recover	*wiedererlangen; sich erholen*
(to) reduce	*herabsetzen, ver-ringern*
(to) refer	*sich beziehen (auf)*
reference	*Bezugnahme, Rück-sprache*
(to) refuse	*abschlagen, sich weigern*
(to) regret	*bedauern*
regular	*regelmäßig*
relation	*Beziehung*
relative	*Verwandte(r)*
relief	*Erleichterung, Hilfe*
remarkable	*bemerkenswert*
remedy	*(Heil-)Mittel*

(to) remember	*sich erinnern*
(to) remind	*erinnern (an)*
(to) remove	*beseitigen, entfernen*
(to) repeat	*wiederholen*
(to) replace	*ersetzen*
(to) reply	*antworten*
report	*Bericht*
representative	*Vertreter*
request	*Bitte, Wunsch*
(to) require	*verlangen, erfordern*
requirement	*Bedürfnis, Erfordernis*
(to) resign	*zurücktreten*
(to) resist	*widerstehen*
resistance	*Widerstand*
respect	*1. Achtung, Ehrfurcht 2. Hinsicht*
responsible	*verantwortlich*
(to) retire	*in den Ruhestand treten*
review	*Kritik*
reward	*Belohnung*
ribbon	*(farbiges) Band*
ripe	*reif*
roots	*Wurzeln [Pl.]*
rope	*Seil, Tau*
rough	*rau, grob*
rude	*unhöflich*
sacrifice	*Opfer*
safety	*Sicherheit*
salary	*Gehalt (Geld)*
satisfactory	*zufriedenstellend*
(to) satisfy	*zufriedenstellen*
(to) save	*retten; aufbewahren*
savings	*Ersparnisse*
(to) saw	*sägen*
scale	*Maßstab*
scarce	*knapp*
(to) scatter	*zer-, verstreuen*
science	*(Natur-)Wissenschaft*
scissors [Pl.]	*Schere*
scratch	*Kratzer, Schramme*
screen	*Bildschirm*
screw	*Schraube*
search	*Nachforschung, Suche*
season	*Jahreszeit*
secret	*Geheimnis*
secretary	*Sekretär(in)*
seed	*Saat, Same*
(to) seize	*ergreifen, packen*
sense	*Sinn, Verstand*
sentence	*Urteil(sspruch)*
separate	*getrennt, abgesondert*
serious	*ernst(haft)*
service	*Bedienung; Dienst*
(to) settle	*sich niederlassen; besiedeln*
settlement	*Siedlung, Niederlassung*

severe	*streng, hart*
(to) sew [ou]	*nähen*
shade	*Schatten*
shame	*Schande; Schamgefühl*
shape	*Form, Gestalt*
shelter	*Schutz*
shore	*Küste, Ufer*
shower	*Dusche*
shy	*schüchtern*
sigh	*Seufzer*
sight	*Anblick*
sincere	*aufrichtig*
single	*einzeln; ledig*
size	*Größe*
skilful	*geschickt, gewandt*
sleeve	*Ärmel*
(to) slide	*gleiten, rutschen*
slight	*schwach, klein, unbedeutend*
(to) slip	*ausrutschen*
slope	*Abhang*
slow motion	*Zeitlupe*
smell	*Geruch*
smooth	*glatt*
snake	*Schlange*
society	*Gesellschaft*
soil	*Erdboden*
solemn	*feierlich*
(to) solve	*lösen, auflösen*
sore	*wund*
sorrow	*Kummer, Schmerz*
soup	*Suppe*
sour	*sauer*
source	*Quelle*
(to) sow [əʊ]	*säen*
speech	*Rede*
(to) spell	*buchstabieren*
(to) split	*auseinander gehen, spalten*
(to) spoil	*verderben, verschandeln*
(to) spread	*ausbreiten, verteilen*
square	*öffentlicher Platz, Viereck*
staff	*Personal*
stain	*Fleck*
statement	*Darstellung; Behauptung*
steady	*stetig; fest; standhaft*
steam	*Dampf*
steering-wheel	*Lenkrad, Steuerrad*
stiff	*steif*
(to) stir	*(sich) rühren, sich regen*
stock	*Vorrat, Lager*
stomach [k]	*Magen*
straight	*gerade*
strength	*Kraft, Stärke*

(to) stretch	*sich erstrecken*
strict	*streng*
strike	*Streik*
stroke	*Schlag, Schlaganfall*
struggle	*Kampf*
study	*Studie*
stupid	*dumm*
subject	*Thema, Gegenstand*
(to) succeed	*Erfolg haben*
(to) suffer (from)	*leiden (an)*
(to) suggest	*vorschlagen*
suggestion	*Anregung, Vorschlag*
(to) suit	*passen*
supply	*Angebot, Vorrat*
(to) supply	*liefern*
(to) support	*ernähren; unterstützen*
(to) suppose	*annehmen, vermuten*
surface	*Oberfläche*
surprise	*Überraschung*
(to) swallow	*schlucken*
(to) swear	*schwören*
(to) sweat [e]	*schwitzen*
(to) sweep	*fegen, kehren*
switch	*Schalter*
sympathy	*Mitgefühl, Mitleid*
tame	*zahm*
task	*Aufgabe*
(to) taste	*schmecken*
tax	*Steuer*
(to) tear	*zerreißen, zerren*
temper	*Stimmung*
tendency	*Tendenz, Neigung*
tender	*zart*
tent	*Zelt*
term	*1. Bedingung* *2. Semester*
than	*als (nach Komparativ)*
thirsty	*durstig*
thorough	*gründlich*
thought	*Gedanke*
thread	*Faden*
(to) threaten	*bedrohen*
throat	*Hals, Kehle*
(to) throw	*werfen*
thus	*so; auf diese Weise*
(to) tie	*binden*
tight	*eng; dicht*
tin	*Zinn*
tip	*1. Spitze* *2. Trinkgeld*
toe	*Zehe*
tongue	*Zunge*
tool	*Werkzeug*
tough	*zäh*
towel	*Handtuch*
trace	*Spur*

track	*(Fuß-)Spur*
treasure	*Schatz*
(to) treat	*behandeln*
treatment	*Behandlung*
trial	*1. Prozess, Verhandlung;* *2. Probe*
tribe	*(Volks-)Stamm*
trunk	*(Baum-)Stamm*
(to) trust	*vertrauen*
tube	*1. Röhre* *2. Londons U-Bahn*
tune	*Lied, Melodie*
(to) twist	*drehen*
ugly	*hässlich*
umbrella	*Regenschirm*
unable	*unfähig*
unemployed	*arbeitslos*
unfavourable	*ungünstig*
unhealthy	*ungesund*
union	*1. Vereinigung* *2. Gewerkschaft*
(to) unite	*(sich) vereinigen*
unknown	*unbekannt*
unless	*wenn nicht*
(to) unload	*entladen*
upper hand	*Oberhand*
(to) urge	*drängen, dringend bitten*
urgent	*dringend*
(to) use	*gebrauchen, nutzen*
useful	*nützlich*
useless	*nutzlos*
usual	*gewöhnlich*
vain	*eitel*
valley	*Tal*
valuable	*wertvoll*
value	*Wert*
variety	*Auswahl, Mannigfaltigkeit*
vegetables [Pl.]	*Gemüse*
veil	*Schleier*
verse	*Strophe*
vessel	*1. Schiff* *2. (Blut-)Gefäß*
victory	*Sieg*
view	*Aussicht*
violent	*gewalttätig; heftig*
virtue	*Tugend*
(to) visit	*besuchen*
(to) vote	*abstimmen; wählen*
voyage	*Schiffsreise*
wage	*Lohn*
want	*Mangel; Bedürfnis*
waste	*Abfall*
(to) waste	*verschwenden*
weak	*schwach*
wealthy	*wohlhabend, reich*
weapon	*Waffe*

weight	*Gewicht*
wet	*nass*
wet paint	*frisch gestrichen*
wheat	*Weizen*
whereas	*wohingegen, während*
whether	*ob*
(to) whisper	*flüstern*
whistle	*Pfeife; Pfiff*
whole	*ganz*
wholly	*gänzlich*
wide	*breit*
wide awake	*hellwach*
widower	*Witwer*
wing	*Flügel*
(to) wipe	*(ab)wischen, (ab)trocknen*
wire	*Draht*
wisdom	*Weisheit*
within	*1. drinnen, im Innern* *2. innerhalb*
within	*innerhalb*
witness	*Zeuge*
(to) wonder	*1. sich fragen* *2. sich wundern über*
woollen	*aus Wolle, wollen*
(to) worry	*sich sorgen, sich ärgern*
worse	*schlechter, schlimmer*
worst	*schlechteste(r, s)*
worth	*wert (sein)*
wound	*Wunde*
(to) wrap	*einpacken, einwickeln*
wrong	*Unrecht*
(to) yield	*1. einbringen, abwerfen* *2. nachgeben*
youth	*Jugend*
zero	*Null*

Britisches und amerikanisches Englisch

deutsche Bedeutung	British English [BE]	American English [AE]
1. Stock	first floor	second floor
Abfall	rubbish	garbage
Apotheke	chemist's	pharmacy, drugstore
Aufzug	lift	elevator
Autobahn	motorway	highway, freeway
Babywindel	nappy	diaper
Bahn	railway	railroad
Benzin	petrol	gas, gasoline
Bonbon	sweet	candy
Briefkasten	post-box	mailbox
Brieftasche	wallet	billfold
Bürgersteig	pavement	sidewalk
Chips	crisps [Pl.]	potato chips [Pl.]
City, Innenstadt	city centre	downtown
ein Auto mieten	hire a car	rent a car
Eis am Stiel	ice lolly	popsicle
Entschuldigung	sorry	excuse me
Erdgeschoss	ground floor	first floor
Fahrplan	timetable	schedule
Führerschein	driving licence	driver's license
Fußball	football	soccer
Fußgängerunterführung	subway	(pedestrian) underpass
Garderobe	cloakroom	checkroom
Gaspedal	accelerator	gas pedal
Geldschein	note	bill
Geschäft	shop	store

deutsche Bedeutung	British English [BE]	American English [AE]
Gleis(e)	rails [Pl.]	tracks [Pl.]
Handtasche	handbag	purse, pocketbook
Herbst	autumn	fall
Hose	trousers [Pl.]	pants [Pl.]
Hosenträger [Pl.]	braces [Pl.]	suspenders [Pl.]
Keks	biscuit	cookie
Kinderwagen	pram	baby carriage
Kino	cinema	movie theater
(Kino-)Film	film	movie
Kofferraum	boot	trunk
Kreisverkehr	roundabout	traffic circle
Limousine	saloon	sedan
Marmelade	jam	jelly
Motorhaube	bonnet	hood
natürlich	of course	sure
öffentliche Verkehrsmittel	public transport	public transportation
Päckchen, Paket	parcel	package
Pommes frites	chips [Pl.]	(French) fries [Pl.]
Portemonnaie	purse	wallet, coin purse
Postleitzahl	postcode	zip code
Privatschule	public school	private school
Punkt	full stop	period, bei Internet-adressen: dot
Radiergummi	rubber	eraser
Rechnung	bill	check
Reißverschluss	zip	zipper
schicken	send	mail
Schrank	cupboard	closet

deutsche Bedeutung	British English [BE]	American English [AE]
Schulferien, Weihnachtsferien	holidays [Pl.]	vacation
Talkshow	chat show	talk show
deutsche Bedeutung	British English [BE]	American English [AE]
Tankstelle	petrol station	gas station
Taschenlampe	torch	flashlight
Taxi	taxi	cab
U-Bahn	underground	subway
Unterhemd	vest	undershirt
Urlaub	holiday	vacation
Warteschlange	queue	line
Watte	cotton wool	cotton
WC	toilet	bathroom, restroom
Weste	waistcoat	vest
Wie bitte?	pardon?, sorry?	excuse me?
Windschutzscheibe	windscreen	windshield
Wohnung	flat	apartment

False Friends

absolvieren	to complete sth.	to absolve	*lossprechen*
Advokat	lawyer, solicitor	advocate	*Verfechter, Befürworter*
Aktion	sale, operation, advertising campaign	action	*Tat, Handlung*
aktuell	topical, current events	actual	*eigentlich, wirklich*
alle Tage	every day	all day	*den ganzen Tag*
Allee	avenue, tree-lined walk	alley	*Gasse, Durchgang*
also	so, therefore	also	*auch, außerdem*
Ambulanz	outpatients' department	ambulance	*Unfallwagen, Krankenwagen*
apart	charming, unusual	apart	*auseinander, abseits*
Argument	point	argument	*Wortwechsel, Streit*
Art	kind, sort, type	art	*(bildende) Kunst*
Artist	(circus) performer, artiste	artist	*Künstler*
ausgesprochen	pronounced, distinct	outspoken	*offen, aufrichtig*
bald	soon	bald	*glatzköpfig, kahl*
bekommen	to receive, to get	to become	*werden*
Billion	trillion	billion	*Milliarde*
Box	loudspeaker, speaker; compartment	box	*Kasten*
brav	well-behaved, good	brave	*tapfer, unerschrocken*
Brief	letter	brief	*kurz, knapp*
Catcher	wrestler	catcher	*Fänger*
Chef	boss, department head	chef	*(Chef-)Koch, Köchin*

City	downtown, city centre	city	Stadt
delikat	delicious; sensitive	delicate	empfindlich, zerbrechlich
dezent	discreet	decent	anständig, ordentlich
Direktion	management	direction	Richtung
Distanz	reserve, coldness	distance	Entfernung
Dom	cathedral	dome	Kuppel(dach)
Dose	box, can, tin	dose	Dosis
Etikett	label, price tag	etiquette	Etikette, Umgangsformen
eventuell	possible	eventual	endlich, schließlich
extravagant	sophisticated	extravagant	übertrieben
Fabrik	factory	fabric	Stoff, Gewebe
fade	bland, tasteless, colourless, boring	to fade	ausbleichen, verblassen
familiär	family-related	familiar	vertraut
Fantasie	imagination	fantasy	Vorstellung, Tagtraum
fast	nearly, almost	fast	schnell
fatal	annoying, awkward, embarrassing	fatal	tödlich, verhängnisvoll
Fleisch	meat	flesh	menschlicher Körper
Formular	form	formula	Formel
Fotograf	photographer	photograph	Fotografie
Fraktion	political party/parliamentary group	fraction	Bruchzahl, Bruchteil
Garage	garage (of a house)	garage	Tankstelle, Autowerkstatt
genial	ingenious, brilliant	genial	witzig, freundlich
Gift	poison	gift	Geschenk
Gymnasium	secondary school [BE] high school [AE]	gym	Turnhalle

Handy	**cellular phone, mobile**	**handy**	*praktisch, nützlich*
Herd	**stove, cooker**	**herd**	*Herde*
hissen	**to hoist / fly a flag**	**to hiss**	*zischen*
Hochschule	**college, university**	**high school**	*Gymnasium, Oberschule*
Kanne	**pot, kettle**	**can**	*Dose*
Kantine	**cafeteria, canteen**	**canteen**	*Besteckkasten, Feldflasche*
Kaution	**bail, deposit**	**caution**	*Vorsicht*
Klosett	**toilet, privy**	**closet**	*Wandschrank, Verschlag*
komfortabel	**luxurious**	**comfortable**	*behaglich, bequem*
komisch	**strange**	**comic(al)**	*lustig*
Kompetenz	**competence, authority, within one's responsibility**	**competent**	*fähig*
Konkurrenz	**competition, competitor**	**concurrence**	*Übereinstimmung*
konsequent	**consistent**	**consequently**	*infolgedessen, folglich*
Kritik	**criticism**	**critic**	*Kritiker*
Mappe	**folder, file, brief-case**	**map**	*Landkarte*
Marmelade	**jam**	**marmalade**	*Orangenmarmelade*
Meinung	**opinion**	**meaning**	*Bedeutung, Sinn*
Menü	**set meal / lunch / dinner, daily special**	**menu**	*Speisekarte*
Mist	**dung**	**mist**	*Nebel*
Mörder	**murderer**	**murder**	*Mord*
Oldtimer	**vintage car, veteran car**	**old timer**	*alter Hase, Veteran*
ordinär	**vulgar**	**ordinary**	*alltäglich, gewöhnlich*
Pension	**boarding house, guesthouse, small hotel**	**pension**	*Rente*

plump	**clumsy, awkward**	**plump**	*mollig, füllig*
positiv	**affirmative**	**positive**	*sicher*
Präservativ	**condom**	**preservative**	*Konservierungsmittel*
Preis	**price**	**prize**	*Siegerpreis*
primitiv	**bare, frugal**	**primitive**	*vorzeitlich*
prinzipiell	**on principle**	**principally**	*hauptsächlich*
Promotion	**doctor's exam**	**promotion**	*Beförderung*
Prospekt	**folder, prospectus**	**prospect**	*Aussicht*
Provision	**commission**	**provision**	*Versorgung, Vorsorge*
Prozess	**law suit, trial**	**process**	*Verfahren*
raffiniert	**clever, cunning, sly**	**refined**	*verfeinert, gebildet*
Rat	**advice**	**rat**	*Ratte*
Rente	**pension**	**rent**	*Miete*
Rezept	**recipe**	**receipt**	*Quittung*
Roman	**novel**	**Roman**	*Römer*
Sekt	**sparkling wine**	**sect**	*Sekte*
sensibel	**sensitive**	**sensible**	*vernünftig*
seriös	**reliable, respectable**	**serious**	*ernsthaft*
sich blamieren	**to embarrass, to disgrace s.b.**	**to blame**	*jdn. beschuldigen*
spenden	**to donate sth.**	**to spend**	*ausgeben*
Stadium	**stage, level**	**stadium**	*Stadion*
Star	**film star, celebrity**	**star**	*Stern*
sympathisch	**nice, pleasant**	**sympathetic**	*verständnisvoll, mitfühlend*
Unternehmer	**business person, employer, entrepreneur**	**undertaker**	*Leichenbestatter*
Warenhaus (Kaufhaus)	**department store**	**warehouse**	*Lagerhalle*

Notizen

Notizen

Notizen

Notizen

Ihre Meinung ist uns wichtig!

Ihre Anregungen sind uns immer willkommen. Bitte informieren Sie uns mit diesem Schein über Ihre Verbesserungsvorschläge!

Titel-Nr.	Seite	Vorschlag

Bitte hier abtrennen

Lernen • Wissen • Zukunft

STARK

Bitte hier abtrennen

Zutreffendes bitte ankreuzen! Die Absenderin/der Absender ist:

- ☐ Lehrer/in
- ☐ Fachadministrator/in
  Fächer:
- ☐ Schuldirektor/in
- ☐ Schulsekretariat
- ☐ Elternteil
- ☐ Schüler/in
- ☐ Sonstiges:

Unterrichtsfächer: **(Bei Lehrkräften!)**

STARK Verlag
Postfach 1852
85318 Freising
DEUTSCHLAND

24-V_Mat

Bitte ausfüllen und im frankierten Umschlag an uns einsenden. Für Fensterkuverts geeignet.

Kennen Sie Ihre Kundennummer? Bitte hier eintragen.

Absender **(Bitte in Druckbuchstaben!)**

Name/Vorname

Straße/Nr.

PLZ/Ort/Ortsteil

Land

Telefon privat

Geburtsjahr

E-Mail

Schule/Schulstempel **(Bitte immer angeben!)**

(Bitte blättern Sie um)